All That I Saw

Sigmund Csicsery

ZALA films

Oakland, California

Published by Zala Films, POB 22833, Oakland, California 94609
www.zalafilms.com

Cover design by George Csicsery. Book design by Joan Olson.

Front cover photo: The author in Red Rock Canyon, Nevada,
November 30, 1974. (Photo by Gabrielle Csicsery)

Library of Congress Cataloging-in-Publication Data is available upon
request.

Printed in the United States of America
First Edition
ISBN-13: 978-1545548233

10 9 8 7 6 5 4 3 2 1

*This book is dedicated to all those
who lost their lives in 1956 fighting for freedom
and an independent Hungary.*

Contents

Preface

THIS BOOK IS written for the children and grandchildren of my brother Miki, who shared many of my early years in Hungary and whom I got to know again after 1956 in Cleveland, Ohio, and California. He died too young, at the age of just forty-two in 1978, but he left five sons who have been a joy to be around as they have grown up, married, and launched careers and lives of their own. Some of them have had children, and by now, some of them have grandchildren. Although I hope that others will discover this volume as well, it is primarily for the large American branch of the Csicsery family descended from Miki.

I was born in the late 1920s and grew up to witness some of the major events of the mid-twentieth century: the horrors of World War II; the rise and fall of dictators and their Nazi, fascist, and Communist ideologies; and the short-lived victory of the 1956 Hungarian Revolution. I survived starvation as a prisoner of war, discrimination as an "enemy of the people," and torture by the Hungarian secret police, and I spent time in prison and as a slave laborer in a coal mine. I was separated from my parents and brothers for more than a decade, took part in the revolution, and then walked to freedom and eventually to a new life in the United States.

This book describes these events and experiences as I saw and remember them. Although I have tried to present facts and avoid emotions, my feelings and prejudices are clearly evident throughout these pages. It would be pointless to conceal what I feel behind a veil of faux objectivity.

I hope this open approach will add to the understanding of these events and of why people behaved as they did under a variety of difficult circumstances. Whenever it was necessary to look to other material to present an accurate account, I relied on carefully selected documents of the time and on other respected published sources, both old and new.

I want to dedicate this book to everyone who raised me, who helped me complete my studies, and who served as an example to emulate. First among these were my parents, who, in addition to giving me an appropriately strict upbringing, sent me to good schools, including the English-Hungarian elementary school in Budapest, the Premonstratensian middle school in Kassa, and the Gábor Áron military school in Nagyvárad. Military school prepared me to survive the ordeals that accompanied the end of World War II and the troubles that ensued over the next twelve years. When hostile government forces pushed me down and tried to eliminate me, I learned not to give in, but instead to stand up and start again.

Among the many others I wish to thank are my aunt Margit néni and her husband, Módly Béla bácsi, who took me in after the war and gave me a home, treating me like one of their own children. They and my godfather, Csicsery Gyula bácsi, and my other uncles and aunts covered my tuition and living expenses during the four years I spent in college in Budapest. Their support made it possible for me to receive my chemical engineering degree.

Once I started my life in the United States, there was a new world to learn about and to grow into. My bosses and coworkers at Monsanto helped me to understand the American way of life and to adapt to it. Professor Herman Pines, my thesis advisor at Northwestern University, was one of the best teachers I ever had. My supervisors, coworkers, and friends at Chevron Research Company provided enormous help in making me feel at home in my new country.

My wife, Gabrielle, whose love and care were my most important supports during the last sixty years, has been by my side since we walked out of Hungary together in 1956. Her devotion and companionship remain a constant source of joy and strength as the years advance. We celebrated our sixtieth wedding anniversary on December 1, 2016.

And finally, I wish to thank my brother George Csicsery, Molly Walker, Sharon Silva, and Joan Olson, who helped me prepare, edit, design, and publish this book.

Sigmund Csicsery
Lafayette, California, May 2017

CHAPTER ONE

Childhood (1929–43)

I WAS BORN on February 3, 1929, in Budapest, Hungary, and was named Zsigmond (Sigmund), after my father, my grandfather, and many other Zsigmonds in the Csicsery clan.

The family had come from the village of Csicser in northeastern Hungary. The 1920 Treaty of Trianon transferred Csicser, though nearly 100 percent Hungarian, from Hungary to the then-new country of Czechoslovakia. On January 1, 1993, with the peaceful dissolution of Czechoslovakia into the Czech Republic and Slovakia, Csicser became part of Slovakia, and today it is called Čičarovce. In 1978, I visited the village (see chapter twenty) for the first time and found the house in which the family had lived beginning in about the twelfth century. My grandfather had been the last of the Csicserys born there. Part of the house had been damaged during World War II, according to the people living in it. On a much later visit, in 2004, the damage remained unrepaired.

My father graduated from the prestigious Ludovika Military Academy in Budapest on August 20, 1920, and became an artillery officer in the Royal Hungarian Army. When I was about three years old, our family moved from a small apartment on Erdélyi Street to an apartment reserved for officers in the Andrássy Barracks on a main ring road, Hungária Körút, on the Pest side of Budapest. I grew up watching the recruits undergoing training, endlessly disassembling mountain cannons, loading the pieces onto the backs of mules, and then reassembling them, ready to fire within minutes. In those years, my father served with the horse-drawn field artillery. He was a good horseman and polo player and won many trophies. All but one, a small silver-plated cup, were lost during the war.

I attended the English-Hungarian Elementary School on Pala Street, on the Buda side of the city, quite far from our home. Children who lived beyond walking distance commuted in taxis, early versions of the school bus.

In the fall of 1938, areas of Czechoslovakia with a Hungarian-speaking majority (including Csicser) were reunited with Hungary, and my father was transferred to Kassa, the largest city in the region. After Christmas, my parents and my little brother, Miklós (Miki), who was born on March 19, 1936, moved to Kassa. I remained in Budapest in order to complete my elementary studies at the school where I had started, moving into my paternal grandparents' house, which was within walking distance of the school. My grandfather went to the movies almost every afternoon and allowed me to accompany him most of the time.

We spent every summer, usually from the end of June until early September, by Lake Balaton, in Balatonszemes, about eighty-seven miles (140 km) southwest of Budapest. My father, who had much less vacation time, was able to join us only on weekends. My maternal grandparents, the Tahys, owned four villas in Szemes. They stayed at the largest of these, the one that was nearest the shore. The three smaller ones and a large orchard were a little farther from the water, up the hill.

The only house with running water was my grandparents', and that water had to be pumped by hand from the well to a tank in the attic. For the other structures, the water was carried from a well. Electricity had been introduced a few years after the villas were built, and the ceiling of each room still had a large hook from which a kerosene lamp could be hung. My grandparents' house had stoves for heating, but the other houses, because they were used only in the summer, did not.

The orchard boasted at least a dozen different varieties of pear tree; many plum trees; apple, cherry, apricot, walnut trees, and hazelnut, raspberry and red currant bushes; and a large fig tree. In 1952, the Communist government confiscated the three small villas and the attached orchard and cut down all of the fruit trees to make space for a summer resort and a ball court for the Russian-Hungarian Friendship Association.

My best childhood memories are from those summer vacations in Balatonszemes. We always stayed in the same small villa. My father usually got up right after sunrise and went fishing off the pier. In addition to the wild and somewhat muddy-tasting common carp species, Lake Balaton had two tasty, specially bred species of carp. One of these, *tükörponty,* or mirror-carp, had only three very large scales on each side of its body, and my father usually had a line or two in the water in the hope of catching one. But he preferred fishing for perch and for the excellent but rare pike-perch (*fogas*). Catching *fogas* is somewhat similar to trout fishing, though more action is required. Sometimes he also caught catfish or pike. After breakfast, we would walk down the hill to the beach to swim until lunchtime. While we were there, the maid would prepare lunch. Our maid—and all of the other maids— swam in the afternoons.

When I was small, I had to take an afternoon nap. The rest of the afternoon, I would play with my numerous cousins and other friends who were also vacationing at Szemes. One of our favorite games was to pretend we were Indians. With a few feathers stuck around our heads, a bow, and arrows made from branches found in the garden, we would go out to hunt cats, pretending they were bison. I don't recall if any of our arrows made a direct hit.

As we grew older, we would go sailing or bicycling. The bicycle trips became longer and longer. At first, we only visited nearby Balatonlelle, Balatonboglár, and Balatonföldvár, but later we took weeklong tours around Lake Balaton or crisscrossed the nearby Bakony Mountains.

· · ·

IN THE FALL of 1939, I joined my parents in Kassa and started my studies at the Premonstratensian High School (Premontrei Gimnázium). At that time in Hungary, eight years of gymnasium followed four years of elementary school.

Kassa is a beautiful city, famous for its medieval Gothic cathedral that contains the tomb of Prince Ferenc Rákoczi II (1676–1735), the leader of one of Hungary's many wars for independence. In 1939, the population of the city was about sixty-five thousand, most of them Hungarians. Six years later, Kassa again became part of Czechoslovakia. When the Communist Czechoslovak government built one of Europe's largest steel mills nearby, the city's population grew to a quarter million. Use of the Hungarian language became illegal in public and discouraged in private. Today, you rarely hear Hungarian spoken on the streets of Kassa.

From September 1939 to early 1940, we lived on the third floor of a huge three-story apartment building in the northern part of the city. When we moved in, we were wondering why some of the rooms had triple-pane windows. We soon found out. Kassa is located in the valley of the Hernád River, at the junction of the plains and the mountains. In winter, icy north winds blow unobstructed from the Carpathian Mountains. Our abode was the first tall structure blocking their fury. We had to close off those rooms and retreat to the part of the apartment that faced south. In the spring of

1940, we moved only a block away to the ground floor of a beautiful villa in a large garden. It was the loveliest home we had ever lived in.

The owners of the house, János and Sári Kiss, and their three daughters, Magda, Márta, and Sárika, occupied the floor above us. Sárika was two years older than my brother Miki, and Márta was two years older than me. We spent our free time with them and their friends. In the spring and summer, we played in the garden; in the winter and when it rained, we were indoors, mostly playing cards. Magda was already an adult and didn't care much about us children.

In 1978, I visited Kassa and went to see our old home. Sári néni and Sárika still lived there, along with Sárika's family. They told me that Magda had died soon after the war, and that Márta and her family were living in Texas. The house in Kassa was demolished in the 1980s and replaced with what I believe is among Europe's ugliest and most poorly constructed small apartment buildings.

My high school teacher was Father Cassian (Kasszián) Holba, a highly educated, wonderful person who could maintain order in an otherwise unruly classroom without ever raising his voice. He immigrated to the United States after the war and served at a Hungarian parish in Akron, Ohio. He became good friends with my parents and officiated at the wedding of my brother Miki. On December 1, 1956, he celebrated my wedding to Gabrielle just a week after we arrived in the United States (see chapter fifteen).

At school, in addition to classes in the Hungarian language, literature, mathematics, physics, chemistry, history, geography, religion, physical education, and music, we had to study Latin for eight years, German from the third year, and either French or Italian from the fifth year. Every morning before classes, except in winter, we had to attend Mass. Classes ended at one or two in the afternoon, and the walk home took twenty minutes. The first thing I did after school was my homework. When I finished, I could read or play or sometimes go to see a movie. If I asked permission to go to the cinema, my father usually checked to see if I had completed my homework and then asked for my Latin or German vocabulary to see how well I had learned the two or three dozen words assigned that day. But he often quizzed me about words we had learned three or four weeks earlier, as well, and I frequently had to return to my room to memorize Latin words instead of going to a movie.

Kassa was also home to a famous theater that offered afternoon performances for students at greatly reduced prices. Tickets were available through our school and were regularly distributed free for good behavior. I saw wonderful performances of Cyrano, Peer Gynt, and other plays, as well as a number of light operettas.

Zsigmond Csicsery and Rózsa Lehoczky, the author's paternal grandparents (Photo by János Berghammer, Munkács; Csicsery family archive)

The Roman Catholic church in Csicser (Photo by the author)

The old family house in Csicser (Photo by the author)

The author's paternal grandfather, General Zsigmond Csicsery (1859–1940), in his Imperial Lifeguards uniform (Photographer unknown; Csicsery family archive)

Zsigmond and Rózsa Csicsery with their three sons (left to right), Gyula, Zsigmond, and László, ca. 1904 (Photographer unknown; Csicsery family archive)

Jakab Tahy (1865–1945), the author's maternal grandfather (Photographer unknown; Tahy family archive)

Jakab Tahy (1865–1945) (Artist unknown; courtesy of Bálint Tahy)

The author's mother, Pálma Csicsery (née Tahy), in 1928 (Photographer unknown; Csicsery family archive)

Pálma Csicsery, ca. 1928 (Photographer unknown; Csicsery family archive)

Zsigmond Csicsery (1900–1962), the author's father, as a lieutenant in the Hungarian army, ca. 1927 (Photographer unknown; Csicsery family archive)

The author with his grandmother, Rózsa, 1929 (Photo by Zsigmond Csicsery)

The author and his mother in 1929 (Photo by Zsigmond Csicsery)

The author at age two (Photo by Zsigmond Csicsery)

The author in 1930 at age one (Photo by Zsigmond Csicsery)

The author on a swing in 1930 (Photo by Zsigmond Csicsery)

The author dressed for play in 1931 (Photo by Zsigmond Csicsery)

The author and his mother at the beach in Balatonszemes, ca. 1931 (Photo by Zsigmond Csicsery)

A Csicsery family portrait, taken on the terrace of their Váralja út home in Buda in 1939, includes (left to right): the author's grandfather, Zsigmond Csicsery (1859–1940), father of László, Gyula, and Zsigmond; the author's first cousin, László Csicsery (1921–41), the only son of Gyula and Ella Csicsery; the author's aunt, Ella Csicsery (née Király), wife of Gyula and mother of László; Pálma Csicsery (née Tahy de tahvár and tarkeö, 1907–2003); the author's brother, Miklós Csicsery (1936–1978); the author's grandmother, Rózsa Csicsery (née Lehoczky de lehota), wife of Zsigmond and mother of László, Gyula, and Zsigmond; the author's father, Zsigmond Csicsery* (1900–1962); the author; and the author's uncle, Gyula Csicsery† (1895–1973). (Photographer unknown; Csicsery family archive)

---

*Zsigmond Csicsery, father of the author and his brothers, Miklós and George, was born in Pécs, southern Hungary, and married Pálma Tahy on June 15, 1927. At the end of World War I, he fought against the Romanians in Transylvania as a member of the Szekler Battalion (Székely Hadosztály). On June 24, 1919, he took part in an unsuccessful coup against the Communist government of Hungary. In 1941 he fought against the Soviet Union in the Ukraine as a lieutenant colonel, successfully leading an artillery division from the Hungarian border of the Carpathian Mountains to the Black Sea while suffering only two casualties. He left Hungary for Germany in 1945, and moved to the United States in 1951, settling in Cleveland, Ohio, where he became a stained-glass painter.

†Gyula Csicsery served in the Royal Hungarian Air Force. In World War I, he fought against the Imperial Russian Army, and in World War II, as a colonel, he fought against the Soviet Union.

*Géza Fejedelem utca 9, Kassa, in 1978
(Photo by the author)*

*The author standing at the signs in Slovak
and Hungarian for the village of Csicser
(Photo by Kornél Eschwig-Hajts)*

*The
Premonstratensian
church in Kassa
(Kosiče) (Photo by
the author)*

CHAPTER TWO

History of Hungary and the Csicsery Family: Some Background

To UNDERSTAND WHAT happened to my family during and after World War II, you must first know something of the history of Hungary itself.

Nomadic Magyars migrated from the east European steppes westward in a little-understood but continuous series of movements spanning several hundred years. In 896, the chiefs of seven Magyar tribes elected Árpád their leader and then crossed the Carpathian Mountains and occupied the Carpathian Basin. (My wife, Gabrielle Szemere, is a direct descendant of Huba, one of these seven chiefs.[1]) At that time, the northwestern Carpathian Basin was part of the Kingdom of Moravia. According to myths recorded in several ancient chronicles, Árpád, via his emissary Kusid (or Kurszán), sent a white horse to Svatopluk, king of Moravia. In return, he asked for a bit of earth, some water, and a tuft of grass. These symbolized the transfer of Svatopluk's domain to the Magyars. In fact, Svatopluk died in 894, two years before the Magyars entered the Carpathian Basin, so if there is any factual basis to the story, the exchange must have been with Svatopluk's sons.

During the next sixty years, Magyar raiders ventured into Germany, France, and northern Italy. The success of these long-range incursions was due in part to Magyar-introduced technical innovations to the military tactics of mounted archery, one of which was stirrups. The stirrup allowed the rider to shoot arrows from a galloping horse. It also proved a significant advantage in hand-to-hand combat. The second innovation was the composite bow, which increased the effective range of arrows. After an initial frontal attack, the Magyars would feign defeat and retreat in apparent disorder. The pursuing cavalry formations would break up during the chase. At a given signal, the Magyars would turn around, stand up in their stirrups, and shoot their arrows.

These forays stopped after two major defeats at the hands of armies dispatched against the Magyars by the German emperor.

Under Grand Prince Géza, who assumed power around 972, and his son, King Saint Stephen (also known as Stephen I), the Magyars converted to Christianity. Saint Stephen (Szent István), a descendant of Árpád, had received his crown from Pope Sylvester II in the year 1000. The Pope also granted him the title Apostolic Majesty, an honorific retained by Hungarian kings for more than nine centuries.

Famous kings of the Árpád dynasty included Saint Ladislaus, also known as Szent László and Ladislaus I, under whose rule (1040–95) the Kingdom of Croatia and Bosnia became part of the Kingdom of Hungary, and Coloman the Learned (Könyves Kálmán), who outlawed the persecution of witches "because they do not exist." The first records of the Csicsery family date from 1107, during the reign of King Coloman (1095–1116). At that time, family members were already living in the village of Csicser.

In 1222, seven years after King John of England put his seal of approval on the Magna Carta, Andrew II (1177–1235), who ruled Hungary from 1205 until his death, issued the Golden Bull to protect the rights of subjects from oppression by their ruler. It became the country's constitution.

During the reign of Andrew's successor, Béla IV (1206–70), the Mongols overran and devastated Hungary, but Béla managed to escape the Mongol army. In 1241, the Great Khan of the Mongols, Ögedei (or Ogotai) (1186–1241) died. The following year, the Mongols withdrew from Hungary. King Béla rebuilt the country, erecting many forts to withstand future Mongol invasions.

The Árpád dynasty ended with the death of Andrew III in 1301. A few years later, the Angevin Charles Robert (1288–1342) became king. During the reign of his son, Louis I (Louis the Great, 1342–82), Hungary became one of the largest countries in Europe. Less than a century after his death, the expansion of Ottoman rule reached the country's borders.

In 1453, the Ottoman sultan Mehmed II (The Conqueror) took Constantinople, capital of the Byzantine Empire. His plan for the conquest of Europe soon brought him into conflict with the Kingdom of Hungary. Mehmed's first objective was to capture Belgrade, the most important border fort guarding the southern entrance to the Carpathian Basin. János Hunyadi, a Transylvanian prince, prepared the defense of the fort well. Mehmed's siege eventually escalated into a major battle. Hunyadi's sudden counterattack overran the Ottoman camp, broke the siege, and forced the wounded sultan to retreat. Hunyadi's victory is considered one of the most important turning points in European history. His capable military leadership delayed the Ottoman onslaught and is believed by Hungarians to have saved Hungary and Europe from the Turks. To commemorate the event, Pope Callixtus III ordered that the bells of every church in Christendom ring at noon each day. This custom was adopted in all Catholic countries, as well as in some Protestant and Orthodox regions. The noonday peal is still heard in most Catholic and some Protestant churches.

Hunyadi's son, King Matthias Corvinus (1443–90), also known as Mátyás az Igazságos (Matthias the Just), was among the most able and enlightened rulers of his time. Under his reign (1458–90), Hungary became the strongest kingdom in central Europe. He created a standing army, promoted the commercial and cultural development of the nation, and introduced the Renaissance to Hungary. A brilliant military leader, Matthias I halted Turkish expansion during his reign. He also waged a war against Emperor Frederick and occupied Lower Austria, including Vienna, between 1482 and 1487.

The first known epic poem in the Hungarian language describes one of the king's wars, the siege of Szabács (Šabac, now in western Serbia). The poem was discovered in the late nineteenth century in the attic of the Csicsery house in Csicser. Although the poem is not signed, its author was most likely a Csicsery ancestor who took part in the siege. In his book *A Szabács viadala*,[2] Imre Samu reprinted the entire poem and analyzed its historical and linguistic significance. The find at the house also yielded several hundred official documents from the late twelfth to the sixteenth century. Today these letters constitute the largest set of medieval documents from a private source in the Hungarian National Archive. Most of the documents discuss legal proceedings, petitions, and judgments related to legal affairs of various Csicsery ancestors, and they are summarized in Part II of *Két Levelesláda Vallomása Nyolc Évszázadról* by Dr. László Oláh.[3]

Matthias I delayed the Turkish threat but failed to eliminate it. In 1526, Sultan Suleiman crushed a Hungarian army at Mohács. Louis II (1506–26) and more than twenty thousand of his men perished there. According to some sources, thirteen members of the Tahy family, my mother's ancestors, were among the casualties. Buda fell to the Ottomans soon after. For the next 150 years, Hungary was divided into three parts: The Habsburgs held the northwestern parts, and the Turks occupied the south-central regions. The eastern part, Transylvania, became independent, gradually evolving into the center of the Magyar movement against Turkish and Habsburg domination. In 1568, the Transylvanian Diet proclaimed freedom of conscience and religious tolerance. The Edict of Torda covered Roman Catholics, Lutherans, Calvinists, and Unitarians. Eastern Orthodox Romanians, Jews, and Muslims were tolerated but not afforded the same rights as adherents of the four Western Christian religions. A subsequent law issued in 1604 guaranteed the equality of all religions and races.

In 1686, a multinational European army liberated Buda and much of Hungary from the Turks. After the Turkish withdrawal, the Austrian Habsburgs took over the whole country, including Transylvania, and the Habsburg emperors were thereafter automatically crowned as Hungarian kings. Unfortunately, they frequently disregarded the Hungarian constitution and persecuted those Hungarians who opposed autocratic Habsburg rule. During the following centuries, several uprisings attempted to rid Hungary of the Habsburgs, or at least force them to obey the constitution. The most famous of these were the 1703–11 uprising led by Francis II Rákóczy and the revolution of 1848. The latter was put down when the Austrians requested Russian help. In late 1849, Russian troops crushed the outnumbered Hungarian rebel army. Reprisals were severe, with thirteen revolutionary generals executed. Eighteen years of oppression and autocratic Austrian rule followed.

Following the Austro-Hungarian Compromise of 1867, Austria and Hungary became a dual monarchy under a common ruler, a union known both as Austria-Hungary and as the Austro-Hungarian Empire. The new constitution granted Hungary full sovereignty over internal affairs and parity with Austria in the conduct of national defense, foreign affairs, and other matters. That same year, the Habsburg emperor Francis Joseph I was crowned king of Hungary.

In 1914, a Serbian terrorist assassinated heir apparent Archduke Franz Ferdinand in Sarajevo. The assassination precipitated World War I. Hungary entered the war as part of the Austro-Hungarian Empire and ended up on the losing side some four years later. The end of the war also marked the end of the dual monarchy. Social and political unrest followed, culminating in a short but brutal Communist rule under Béla Kun. My uncle, the naval officer László Csicsery, led a mutiny of the Danube flotilla in a futile attempt to overthrow the Communists and died in the fighting. Later, in 1919, Admiral Miklós Horthy de Nagybánya organized a counterrevolutionary army and assumed power as regent after the Communists were defeated.

On June 4, 1920, the victors of World War I imposed on Hungary the debilitating Treaty of Trianon. Hungary lost more than two-thirds of its land and population, with the country shrinking from 125,641 square miles (325,409 sq km) to 35,919 square miles (93,030 sq km), and the prewar population of nearly 21 million dropping to only 7.6 million people. The northern area became part of the newly created Czechoslovakia, Romania received Transylvania and part of the plains adjoining it, and Yugoslavia incorporated the country's southern parts and Croatia. Even Austria was granted a small part (Burgenland), and Italy got the port city of Fiume (today Rijeka).

Although the peace treaty guaranteed autonomy to the Hungarian minorities living within the successor states, this never became a reality. Even today, the more than three million Hungarians living in Slovakia, Romania, and Serbia have no autonomy, and Hungarians remain the largest minority populations living in other countries in Europe. The treaty turned 35 percent of the Hungarian people into second-class citizens of the successor countries,[4] and in several areas, they became the victims of ethnic cleansing. The new rulers confiscated the property and houses of tens of thousands of Hungarians and forced many to denounce their nationality. If they refused, they lost their jobs. Many were persecuted for speaking Hungarian in public, and countless Hungarian schools and other institutions were closed. Not surprisingly, about 350,000 Hungarians left all of their possessions and fled to what was left of Hungary. As noted earlier, the Treaty of Trianon awarded Csicser, the Csicsery family's ancestral village, to Czechoslovakia.

In addition to territorial losses, the Treaty of Trianon rendered Hungary defenseless against her neighbors by limiting her army to thirty-five thousand and prohibiting the building of two-way railway lines and bridges spanning major rivers near border areas. The treaty also required Hungary to pay enormous sums in restitution to the victors and imposed severe economic sanctions.

American President Woodrow Wilson wanted to draw the new borders based on plebiscites, but his views were disregarded. This was one of the factors that resulted in the US Congress refusing to ratify the treaty.

Modifying the Treaty of Trianon and the return of most of the lost territories became Hungary's prevailing policy goal during the 1920s and 1930s. In every school, from first grade on, students were exposed daily to the revisionist slogan No, No, Never (a play on the word *trianon,* which in Latin means "three times no"). The covers of the school notebooks displayed these words together with a map showing Hungary's old and new borders. Students had to recite a short daily prayer: "I believe in one God, I believe in one Homeland, I believe in eternal divine justice, and I believe in the resurrection of Hungary."

Collaboration with Germany promised a possible way (perhaps the only way) for a revision of the Treaty of Trianon. And indeed, Hitler rewarded Hungary's friendly policy. In 1938, he agreed to return part of Czechoslovakia and in 1939 all of Ruthenia (Carpatho-Ukraine) to Hungary. The following year, Hungary recovered the northern half of Transylvania. Finally, in April 1941, Hungary occupied some of the territories that had been awarded to Yugoslavia by the treaty.

A few days after the bombing of Kassa on June 26, 1941, Hungary, believing that the bombers were Soviets, declared war on the Soviet Union. My father took part as a battalion commander in the early months of the campaign. Three years later, after the Hungarian army suffered devastating losses on the Russian front, the government tried to negotiate with the Allied powers. The Germans quickly learned about these attempts to arrange a ceasefire. On March 19, 1944, German troops occupied the country and installed a pro-German puppet regime but did not immediately remove the regent, Admiral Horthy. Roughly seven months later, on October 7, the Soviet army invaded Hungary. Horthy's attempt on October 15, 1944, to stop the fighting and surrender to the Allies ended with his arrest by the Germans and the installation of a Hungarian fascist government that immediately turned against all dissidents, especially the Jews. Several hundred thousand Jews were either killed or deported to German death camps.

On Christmas Eve of the same year, the Soviet army surrounded Budapest. The siege, which was brutal, lasted seven weeks, with the Soviet troops overcoming the last German and Hungarian defenders on February 13, 1945. Most of the city lay in ruins. The once-beautiful Royal Palace was in ruins, and all seven bridges across the Danube had been destroyed by the Germans.

The last Hungarian village fell to the Russians on April 4, 1945, and the war in Europe ended in early May. In 1947, a new peace treaty restored the frontiers created by the Treaty of Trianon. Kassa and Csicser again became part of Czechoslovakia, Romania regained northern Transylvania, and Yugoslavia took back what it had lost in 1941, murdering thousands of innocent Hungarians in the process. Ruthenia (Kárpátalja) became part of the Soviet Union.

After the war, the Independent Smallholders' Party won Hungary's first free elections. During the following years, the Communist Party, with the help of Soviet occupation forces, eliminated all non-Communist politicians, and by May 1949, Hungary had become a satellite of the Soviet Union. The Communist Party established complete control over all aspects of life, nationalizing most industries, all of the banks, most other institutions, and most church schools. Mátyás Rákosi, the general secretary of the Hungarian Communist Party, was a de facto dictator. The Communist Party–controlled secret police (variously called ÁVO or ÁVH) arrested hundreds of priests and nuns who opposed these actions. József Cardinal Mindszenty, the primate of Hungary, was also arrested and, in a sensational show trial, was sentenced to life imprisonment. Peasants were persuaded to collectivize, that is, give their land to a collective farm, and those who refused to do so were persecuted and their lands confiscated. Tens of thousands of opponents of the Communist regime were sentenced to labor camps (I was among them), deported from their homes (my future wife, Gabrielle, and her family), or imprisoned in one of the Hungarian Gulags (again, I was among them). Hundreds were executed or taken to Siberian death camps.

Following Stalin's death in 1953, and during the subsequent "de-Stalinization" under Khrushchev, the power of the secret police was curbed. Widespread changes affected all aspects of life in the Soviet sphere. In Hungary, the dictator Rákosi was replaced by a moderate leader, Imre Nagy, who immediately instituted sweeping reforms. But Rákosi retained the key position of First Secretary of the Communist Party and soon ousted Nagy.

Popular discontent erupted in Budapest on October 23, 1956. At first, university students demonstrated against compulsory Russian language and Marxism-Leninism courses and, along with members of the writers' union, expressed their sympathy with the simultaneous Polish anti-Soviet movement. Within hours, the students were joined by workers. Army troops that were ordered to quell the demonstrations joined them instead. The people elected Imre Nagy chairman of the Council of Ministers. He suspended the one-party system and promised free elections. He also pledged economic reforms, freed Cardinal Mindszenty, demanded the withdrawal of Soviet forces, denounced the Warsaw Pact, and proclaimed Hungary a neutral state.

The Communist leadership, still loyal to Moscow, responded to Nagy's actions by asking the Soviet occupying forces to reestablish their rule. On November 3, the Soviets invited Pál Maléter, the new Hungarian minister of defense, to negotiate and then promptly arrested him and his staff. That night, Soviet troops invaded the country with about four thousand tanks, brutally ending the revolution. A new Communist dictatorship was set up, with János Kádár as chairman of the Council of Ministers. Hundreds of Hungarians were executed, thousands more were imprisoned, and nearly a quarter million fled to the West (see chapter fourteen for a more detailed account of what happened in 1956, and my experiences during that time).

Eventually, Kádár realized that for his regime to survive, he would have to decrease terror and improve living standards. By the 1970s, Hungary had become the least oppressed of all the Soviet-occupied countries, and Kádár's more tolerant system had been dubbed Goulash Communism. Relations with the West steadily improved, and a limited form of private enterprise was encouraged. Hungary was the first of the so-called satellite countries to relax censorship and establish a multiparty system that eventually led to the fall of Communism. The opening of the Hungarian border to Austria for East Germans to escape to the Free World in 1989 was an important milestone in this chain of events—a move that helped lead to the fall of the Berlin Wall and the end of East Germany (the German Democratic Republic).

In 1990, in the nation's first free elections in forty-five years, a coalition of center-right parties won a parliamentary majority. Nine years later, Hungary joined NATO, and in May 2004, Hungary became a member of the European Union.

CHAPTER THREE

World War II (1939–45)

In September 1939, Germany invaded Poland, which marked the beginning of World War II. Poland and Hungary had enjoyed good relations since the Middle Ages, so when German and Russian forces pushed into Poland, Hungary opened its borders to both Polish civilians and soldiers. Thousands of Polish refugees flooded into the country. In the town of Balatonboglár, which I had visited as a youngster during my summer vacations at Lake Balaton, the Hungarian government set up a high school for Polish children. The government also helped Polish soldiers escape to England, from where they could continue to fight the Germans.

Although our family witnessed all of these events, our lives were not significantly affected by the first two years of the war. But that would change.

In the summer of 1941, Hitler attacked the Soviet Union, and German troops were allowed to pass through Hungary on their way to Russia. Although Hungary did not at first participate in the invasion, that did not last long. At noon on June 26, 1941, low-flying unmarked airplanes bombed Kassa. My brother Miki and I were home playing in the garden when we saw the planes circling above us. A short time later, we heard a few dozen very loud explosions. About thirty bombs had fallen on and around the new main post office. One bomb that hit the building knocked out the telephone center. Altogether about thirty people died. We had some newly hatched chickens that were drinking from a pot when the bombs went off. The thunderous blasts so frightened the chicks that all but one fell into the water and drowned.

My father was working in Budapest at the time and did not learn about the bombing until late in the afternoon. He immediately tried calling us, but the long-distance operator told him that all phone connection with Kassa was down because the "city is in ruins." He took the first available train to Kassa and was much relieved to discover that the news was greatly exaggerated. Although life in Kassa resumed for the moment, the bombing would soon prove to have tragic and fateful consequences.

Who were these attackers? We still don't know for sure. Some thought the bombing was a German provocation to coerce Hungary into joining its offensive against the Soviet Union. Others blamed the Czechs, the Slovaks, the Romanians, or some vengeful Yugoslav pilots.[5] The authorities announced that the bombers had come from Russia, and a few days later, the Hungarian government declared war on the Soviet Union. In recent times, a number of historians have given credence to the theory that the bombers were Soviet but had strayed from their intended target, a city in Slovakia only 19 miles (30 km) from Kassa. At the time, Slovakia was already at war against the Soviet Union.

My father was among the first Hungarian troops sent to the front. He was an artillery battalion commander, and his battalion consisted of two batteries of four 150mm howitzers each. The howitzers were so heavy that the barrels had to be transported separately from their carriages and reassembled before use. Heavy-duty Italian-manufactured Pavesi vehicles pulled the two parts. The Pavesi was the strangest-looking machine I had ever seen. Designed for desert use, it had enormous wheels and consisted of two equal-size halves with fixed axles. Large horizontal, partial cogwheels connected the two units. Moving these cogwheels on each other turned the front half left or right relative to the rear part, thus steering the vehicle.

Every large military unit had a symbol that was painted on each vehicle. A white elephant was the symbol of my father's battalion. I still own a small, white marble elephant that belonged to him.

The German blitzkrieg against the Russian army was initially successful. Combined German, Hungarian, and Romanian forces inflicted enormous losses on the retreating Russian units. They advanced as fast as possible on the sometimes dusty, sometimes muddy Russian roads. Except when it encountered some resistance and had to fight, my father's unit was almost constantly on the move. By late summer, it had reached the Black Sea near Odessa.

On August 10, 1941, my paternal grandmother passed away at the age of seventy. My father was allowed to leave his unit to attend her funeral and spend a few days with us. We were very happy to see him, and he told us many interesting stories. At the time, he was still optimistic about the defeat of Communism because Hungarian and German casualties had remained low. His unit had suffered only two fatalities during the whole time the battalion was in Russia.

At the end of the summer, the battalion was recalled to Kassa. My father's performance was rewarded with the Knight's Cross, with swords on the war ribbon of the Hungarian Order of Merit (Magyar Érdemrend Lovagkeresztje a Kardokkal a Hadiszalagon). The ribbon acknowledged that he received this decoration during a war, while the swords signified that he had earned it in combat. He was also presented with the German Iron Cross. Sometime later, he was transferred to the Ministry of Defense in Budapest. One of his tasks was to organize self-propelled artillery units. He saw no more combat during the war.

That was fortunate. The next three winters were extremely severe. The German armies lost the battle of Stalingrad and suffered other setbacks. During the battle, the Second Hungarian Army, about two hundred thousand soldiers, was assigned to hold the line at the great bend of the Don River. It was midwinter and unusually cold when the Russians attacked with fresh troops. Most of the inadequately armed and poorly equipped Hungarian soldiers were killed or captured. Many froze to death. The effect of these huge losses was widespread, as there were few in Hungary who did not lose a relative or a friend. It is estimated that of the two hundred thousand soldiers and the fifty thousand Jewish laborers attached to the army, only forty thousand men ever returned to Hungary.

Although the actual fighting was still far from our borders, the war started to affect everyday life. Sugar, flour, bread, and lard—at that time in Hungary, most people cooked with lard instead of vegetable oil—were rationed. Quite often, we could not purchase any meat.

Becoming a Cadet

IN 1943, WHEN I was fourteen years old, I was accepted as a cadet by the artillery school in Nagyvárad. In addition to all of the subjects taught at civilian schools, we were trained to become officers by the age of eighteen. The school was named after Gábor Áron, a self-taught Transylvanian metalworker who manufactured cannons for the revolution of 1848. He was killed in action in July 1849 while fighting against the tsarist invading forces.

We freshmen started our studies a few weeks before the rest of the students because we had to go through basic training. Our hair was cut. We learned how to march in step, how to handle and clean our rifles, how to take care of our clothing, how to clean our boots "so not a speck of dust remained," and most important, how to obey orders. For me, this was very hard. I had to go from being a spoiled civilian kid who spent most of his free time reading and playing to being a tough, well-disciplined soldier whose highest ambition was to keep his boots and rifle spotless. After some months, I got used to this new life and even started to enjoy it.

We had exercises and classes from daybreak until dinnertime. Discipline for first-year cadets was imposed not only by officers and teachers but also by our upperclassmen room commanders. The slightest infringement, such as missing a shirt button or a speck of mud on your boot, was punished by up to a hundred push-ups or by revocation of Sunday afternoon leave (*kimenő*), the only time we were allowed to go to the city to see a movie or to eat one or two *krémes* in a patisserie. I still remember the name Japport Cukrászda, Nagyvárad's most famous pastry shop.

During the fall of 1943, my family moved from Kassa to Budapest. We rented a small apartment in Buda, on Királyhágó Street, not too far from the Southern Railway Station. Christmas vacation was the first time I went home. My joy at being with my parents and brother was tempered only a little by having my hair completely shorn at school as punishment for some disciplinary problem.

On March 19, 1944, all of the students and officers were told to assemble in the school's auditorium. Our commander, Colonel Géza Paletta, informed us that the German army, having learned that the Hungarian government was negotiating an armistice with the Allies, had occupied Hungary overnight. The colonel did not yet know what this meant for the school. Within a short time, however, the Germans installed a German-friendly government but left Miklós

Horthy as head of state. The Gestapo, Nazi Germany's secret police, arrested many politicians and started the deportation of Jews. Up until then, the Allies had not bombed Hungary, but a few days later, on Palm Sunday, the bombing of Budapest began. Rumor has it that one of the first bombs hit the statue of George Washington. I was in Budapest on Easter vacation when the Allied planes carpet bombed a German airplane factory on the island of Csepel, south of Budapest, that manufactured Messerchmitt Me 201 planes. My father was sent to inspect the damage, and he took me with him. The devastation was incredible. This was my first close contact with the war.

The Germans soon requested that the Hungarian army give them all military barracks not in use. To save at least a handful of these buildings from German use, our school sent classes to some of the unoccupied barracks and other institutions.

The student body at Nagyvárad was divided into four "batteries," each with its first-, second-, third-, and fourth-year students. Our class, which was called 3/1, that is, third battery, first year, was sent to Nagykároly to occupy a military school where the students were already on summer vacation. It was in a beautiful former castle in a large park. The month I spent there was the most pleasant part of my short and inglorious military career.

After that memorable month, we held maneuvers at Hajduhadház. For a few weeks, we fired real ammunition from machine guns and 105mm howitzers. Although we were barely fifteen years old, we felt like grown-up soldiers—and we liked that.

The year I spent at military school changed me. I learned discipline and made many lifelong friendships. The most important lesson I and my fellow students learned was that regardless of the hopelessness or danger of a situation, we should never lose courage and never give up. Training at the school in Nagyvárad helped me and most of my schoolmates to survive the twelve very difficult years that would follow.

• • •

BY MIDSUMMER 1944, Hungary had somehow managed to wiggle out of German control. Miklós Horthy even replaced the pro-German prime minister and the rest of his government. The most important task for the new prime minister was to negotiate the country's surrender to the Russians. On the morning of October 15, 1944, Horthy went on the radio to announce that Germany had lost the war, Hungary would surrender to the Allies, and all fighting should cease. His attempt was unsuccessful. After a brief battle, the Germans arrested him and installed a Nazi government that continued the war and intensified the extermination of the Jews.

Army units close to the front lines laid down their arms and went over to the Russians. But those in German-controlled regions had to continue fighting. Desertions became widespread. My father was reassigned to the newly created Homeland Army commanded by General Kálmán Ternegg, his top commander throughout most of his career. At first, the Homeland Army headquarters was in Balatonfüred, a beautiful resort on the north shore of Lake Balaton. During the summer, my mother, Miki, and, after August, I stayed in Balatonszemes. At the end of October, we all joined my father in Balatonfüred. As the Russians advanced, we were relocated to Rum in western Hungary, staying at the castle of Count Móricz Széchényi.

In the meantime, my school had relocated to Sümeg, a little town in western Hungary north of Lake Balaton, and to the nearby village of Csabrendek. I managed to rejoin the school at the very end of 1944. I said goodbye to my parents and Miki and left Rum on December 29, 1944. We would not see one another again for twelve years.

The news from the Soviet-occupied parts of the country was horrifying. Soviet soldiers killed and raped thousands, robbed and took whatever they could carry, and deported tens of thousands to Russia. This prompted many thousands of Hungarians to escape to Austria and Germany. My family ended up in Haimbuch, a little Bavarian village. My brother György was born in the nearby city of Regensburg on March 17, 1948. Soon after György's birth, my parents and my two brothers moved to Herrenalb, a spa town near Baden-Baden in the Black Forest. Both my mother and my father found employment there with the French-occupying forces. My father, always a very talented artist, became a draftsman, and my mother, who spoke French, became a typist-stenographer. After less than three years in Herrenalb, they immigrated to the United States, arriving in New York City aboard a troop-carrying Liberty ship on January 11, 1951. They soon settled in Cleveland, Ohio.

The Flight to Germany

FIVE DAYS AFTER I rejoined my unit in Sümeg, our class, now seasoned second-year cadets, and the new freshmen boarded a train and left Hungary. Our group was relocated to Grossborn-Westfahlenhof (now Borne Sulinowo, Poland), a large German artillery-training center in the northeastern corner of Germany. The train journey took a week, and we spent two more weeks unloading our equipment and belongings.

The day we completed this task, the Russian army broke through German defense lines to our east and rapidly approached Grossborn. We fled on foot, leaving almost all of our belongings behind. We fabricated little sleds from bed planks, loaded some of our warm clothes and food on them, and started westward on snow-covered roads. At each hill, we had to discard excess clothing and even some food to lighten our sleds. On the first day, we dragged our sleds along until well past midnight. At night, the temperature dropped to −40°F (−40°C). A blizzard started a few days later, and we could not continue in the deep snow. Fortunately, the severe weather also slowed the Russian advance. We waited and rested three days in the village of Woltensdorf. When the blizzard eased, we resumed our westward trek. A second train that was supposed to bring the third-year cadets from our school to Grossborn was rerouted to Wangerin, a small city east of Stettin (Szczecin, Poland). On January 28, 1945 we met our fellow cadets there. Our commanders accommodated all of us in the already crowded freight cars of their train. Our long walk was over.

We spent a few days at a railroad station near Tempelhof, a suburb of Berlin. Here, on February 1, we survived one of the largest bombing raids on Berlin. We then wasted a few days in Jütterbog, where I celebrated my sixteenth birthday. On February 6, we finally arrived in Eger (Cheb, Czech Republic).

The next two months in Eger were surprisingly peaceful, and we resumed our studies. However, after the end of March, the Allies started bombing the city. In mid-April, our commanders decided to relocate us to the safety of a forest near Tirschenreuth, a small city in Bavaria, which was a good day's walk from Eger. Once in the forest, we set up tents and waited for the United States Army. A week later, on April 22, 1945, American troops occupied Tirschenreuth without opposition.

A Prisoner of War for Six Months

THE AMERICAN TROOPS occupying Tirschenreuth did not ask whether we were Hungarians or Germans, whether we were children or grown-ups, whether we were students or soldiers. They simply loaded all of us, without our belongings, onto big trucks and took us to prisoner-of-war camps.

The next half year was the most miserable period of my life. In the first camps—in Bayreuth, Kulmbach, and the infamous camp of Bad Kreuznach that had close to a million prisoners of war—we slept on the ground, rain or shine. We had no tents, blankets, ground sheets or mattresses, not even raincoats. And we received very little food. After a few weeks, we looked like skeletons. We were so emaciated that it was hard to stand and walk. Although some of us contracted tuberculosis, no one died. We were then taken to France. There we slept in tents, but the starvation continued. We languished for three weeks near Foucarville in Normandy, two months near Cherbourg, and another month in Mailly-le-Camp. Our group was more fortunate than those guarded by French troops, however. Theft of food and supplies by French officials had disastrous consequences. According to some reports, nearly half of the young Hungarian prisoners died of starvation in the prisoner-of-war camp at Poitiers. My best friend and relative, Árpád Maléter, was one of them. In *Other Losses,* James Bacque presents detailed descriptions of American prisoner-of-war camps in Germany and France.[6]

In mid-October 1945, the United States Army returned most of us to Hungary. The train ride home took more than a week, and we were released in the southern Hungarian city of Kaposvár. In a diary I started when we left Hungary, I described the story of our trip to Grossborn, our subsequent flight to escape capture by the Russians, our relatively peaceful months in Eger, and the bitter six months of captivity.[7]

CHAPTER FOUR

Living in Soviet-Occupied Hungary (1945–51)

I ARRIVED HOME in late 1945 to find Hungary a devastated country. Soviet soldiers were confiscating everything they could from the civilian population: cars and trucks, horses and cattle, most of the locomotives and rolling stock, as well as clothes, furniture, and other private property. They were especially fond of wristwatches. Even some factories were dismantled and most of the machinery carried off to the Soviet Union.

In October 1945, when we prisoners of war had been released in Kaposvár, no trains were running anywhere in the entire country. We were told that the lack of coal was the reason. I walked toward Lake Balaton and arrived in Balatonszemes two days later. I stayed there for some weeks with my grandmother. My grandfather had died the previous winter, soon after the Russian army's arrival. No one knew where my parents were. A few weeks later, I received news that they had survived the war and were in Bavaria.

When I learned that Gyula bácsi, my uncle and godfather, and his wife, Ella néni, had returned to Budapest from Austria, I moved to his apartment on Mészáros Street, in Buda. The building, which was one of the last ones captured from the Germans, was in ruins. The entire roof and attic, and the floor above Gyula bácsi's apartment, were missing. I could see the sky from my bed. When it rained or snowed, Gyula bácsi and I would cover the hole with an old tent to keep me dry. After each snowfall, we would climb up to where the floor above used to be and shovel the snow away. There was no way to heat my room. The staircase had been destroyed, so we climbed to the upper floors on a wooden board.

During the winter of 1945–46, Budapest starved. The food stores were empty. We were hungry all the time. At several railroad stations, returning prisoners of war received free lunch, usually pea soup, for three days following their arrival. I was soon "arriving home" every fourth day at a different railroad station for my free lunch. Once I had completed the entire circuit, I would start again at the beginning. I got away with this for a while, until a friendly sergeant recognized me and warned that I could get into trouble if I continued.

I went to Somogy County with a full backpack to barter salt and some old clothing Gyula bácsi had saved in exchange for food. Very few passenger trains were running because there wasn't much fuel, so I had to travel on freight cars. I started by going to Balatonszemes, to the home of Béla bácsi, my maternal uncle. There I borrowed a bicycle from his wife, Dóra néni, and continued on to Somogyvár, a village about thirty-eight miles (60 km) south of Lake Balaton. I managed to trade the salt and the clothing with farmers I knew there and returned to Budapest with a lot of flour, lard, bacon, and a whole baked goose. That helped us for a while.

Later that fall, I reenrolled in high school. First, I had to pass exams to prove that I was caught up with what I had missed during the last year of the war and subsequent captivity. Latin was the most difficult because it was not taught at military school. I had to master two years of material in just two months. A good friend's mother helped me study, and somehow I passed all of the exams.

My school, the Werbőczy (now Petőfi Sándor) Gimnázium, was only a ten-minute walk from Gyula bácsi's apartment. It had been severely damaged during the siege of Budapest, and parts of the building were in ruins. The windows in most of the classrooms had no glass. In early spring, the authorities declared the building unsafe and condemned it. We moved on to share classrooms with students from the Rákóczi Gimnázium on Marczibányi Square. They occupied the classrooms during the morning; we used them in the afternoon.

The majority Independent Smallholders' Party nominally governed the country. However, the minority Communist Party, with only 11 percent of the vote but with the overt help of the occupying Soviet army, started to control every aspect of life. The Catholic Church, and its head archbishop, Cardinal József Mindszenty, primate of Hungary, became their primary targets. The cardinal actively resisted the Communist takeover by delivering speeches everywhere. One day he was scheduled to speak at noon at the Krisztina church, which was near our school. A very stern warning from the Ministry of Education forbade us to attend. As I remember, every class at our school went to hear him. Even the Protestants in our class were there. Our director was punished, and the students received "second degree warnings," a written note that was supposed to affect our final grades and that our parent or guardian had to sign. However, we sensed that our director and teachers were very proud of us, as was Gyula bácsi of me when he signed my note. In the end, nobody's grades suffered.

In our area, Cardinal Mindszenty performed the confirmation ceremony, and so it was he who confirmed me at the Városmajor church. A pretty blonde girl from a nearby girls' high school and I were selected to deliver short valedictory speeches to the cardinal after the ceremony. As I started to recite my carefully memorized speech, the girl got cold feet, started to cry, and ran out of the room. It was rather embarrassing, but I managed to complete my task. After that, the cardinal exchanged a few words with me. I was in seventh heaven!

One early victim of the state's vindictiveness was General Kálmán Ternegg, or Kálmán bácsi, as he was called by most people in the Hungarian army. He was my father's supervisor throughout most of my father's career. During the last decade or so of his service, General Ternegg was inspector of artillery, in charge of all artillerymen. He was a competent and popular leader. My parents and everyone who served under him liked him. After the war, the Communist Party declared him a war criminal and brought him back from West Germany in handcuffs. I attended his trial at the parliament building. His crime was issuing an order for deserters to be shot, and the outcome was predictable: fifteen years in prison. He died just before he was to be released. During an intermission at the show trial, while I was standing with friends in the hallway, Mátyás Rákosi, secretary of the Communist Party and future dictator of Hungary, walked by us. He walked between two tall, stern-looking bodyguards. Each man kept one hand in a pocket.

Around this time, Gyula bácsi contracted tuberculosis. The near-starvation conditions and living in an unheated home were likely contributing factors. His illness meant that I could no longer stay in his home, and he even forbade me to visit him, fearing possible contagion. Margit néni, a maternal aunt, and her husband, Béla bácsi (Béla Módly), took me in and treated me very well during the following years. Meanwhile, Gyula bácsi's health deteriorated rapidly. At the last minute, the discovery of two wonderful drugs, PAS (*para*-Aminosalicylic acid) and INH (Isoniazid or isonicotinylhydrazine), saved his life. In a relatively short time, he regained his former strength.

At the Technical University

IN JUNE 1947, I passed the *matura*, a difficult examination covering the curricula of the last four years of high school, with the best possible grades. This allowed me to apply for chemical engineering at the prestigious Technical University of Budapest. A challenging entrance examination led to the selection of between eighty and ninety students out of the four hundred applicants. I was among the lucky ones who passed. The Communist Party reserved an additional dozen seats for party members. They were not required to take an entrance examination.

I started my studies at the university in September 1947. During the first year, my tuition was greatly reduced because my parents were not in the country. However, by the fall of 1948, the Communists had gained full control of the university. When my tuition application was not returned, I went to the accounting office to inquire. The clerk in charge and I lived in the same building and knew each other well. He said, "Let's see." I saw his expression change when he got to my application. A note in huge red letters said: "His parents live in the West. Maximum tuition!" After he showed this to me, he said, "You did not see anything, did you?" I assured him that I did not. I also understood that from now on, I would have a very hard time at the university. To survive I would have to devote all of my time to studying to ensure that I received the best possible grades.

At the end of the war, the Russians had captured my mother's youngest brother, Kálmán, and had taken him to Russia as a prisoner of war. One evening in early 1948, he appeared at Margit néni and Béla bácsi's doorstep. He had survived Russian captivity but was emaciated. He moved in with Margit néni and Béla bácsi, where he regained his strength and eventually landed a good job at the Ministry of Agriculture. He married Karola Ágay, a famous soprano with the Budapest opera. Sometime later he was fired from his job because of a careless remark about a coworker's decision to join the Communist Party just a few days after the start of the Korean War. His question, "At the end of the season?" referred to a widespread optimistic belief that the United Nations intervention in Korea would bring down Communism and Hungary would regain her independence. After that he worked in western Hungary as a surveyor.

Margit néni and Béla bácsi's fifth child, Margit, was born on June 1, 1947. They chose me to be her godfather. I felt honored, as I was only eighteen. Margit néni's sixth child, Évi, was born on February 5, 1949. As the two little girls grew older, I often played with them, and we developed a very strong relationship. However, with two new children, the apartment became crowded, so I moved to the nearby Szent Imre Kollégium, a Roman Catholic dormitory that also provided meals. My grandmother, Béla bácsi, and my other uncles contributed the money necessary to make my move possible and also covered my increased tuition at the university.

By the fall of 1948, it was obvious that the Communists would soon take over the country. The leaders and important members of the Independent Smallholders' Party were accused of being either agents of the Western powers or reactionaries, or they were simply arrested by the secret police or the Soviet army. Some of them ended up in the Gulag camps in Siberia. István Csicsery-Rónay, a close relative and an elected Independent Smallholders' Party representative, was one of those arrested. In 1949, he managed to escape to the West and settled near Washington, DC. He returned to Hungary in 1991 and remained there until his death in 2011. Following the return of some of his family property, he spent part of the year in Budapest and the rest in Zala, near Lake Balaton, residing in the former manor house owned by his grandfather, Mihály Zichy, the famous nineteenth-century painter.

The Communists called 1948 The Year of the Turnaround (*A Fordulat Éve*). It was the beginning of a most brutal and oppressive dictatorship. When the hopelessness of the situation became obvious, thousands decided to leave the country and try their luck in Austria, Germany, or in some other Western country. Crossing the border to Austria wasn't easy, and not without serious consequences if you were caught. Nevertheless, it was still possible to leave through the end of 1948. Most would-be escapees hired a paid agent. In the fall of 1948, Béla bácsi's son Zoltán, who is six months older than I, left Hungary.

When Béla bácsi received news that Zoltán had safely reached Austria, he invited my grandmother and my other uncles for a meeting. He told us that he would be able to hire the same agent to engineer my escape. As such a step would be quite risky, he wanted a joint family decision about whether I should leave or stay. The arguments for both options were powerful. If I left, I could join my parents and brothers. If I remained in Hungary, I could finish my studies. The opinion of my uncle Feri bácsi was that I should leave the country only after completing my studies. Indeed, in those years, chemical engineering was considered the best of all professions. My other uncles suggested that I should leave Hungary as soon as possible and try to continue my education in Germany. But then, after a protracted discussion, we decided that I should leave the country only after graduating. Who knows what my life would have been like if we had decided otherwise?

A few months later, at the end of 1948, the Communists closed the border with double barbed-wire fences, minefields, and watchtowers. The fabled Iron Curtain described by Winston Churchill became a physical reality. Chances of successfully crossing it became extremely low. Most of those who attempted the escape were either killed by landmines, shot, or captured by the border police. Those who were caught were imprisoned.

Destruction of the Roman Catholic Church was the Communists' next objective. The Communist-controlled press attacked Cardinal Mindszenty almost daily. The government took over almost all of the parochial schools and convents and imprisoned many priests and nuns. My Catholic dormitory, the Szent Imre Kollégium, was on the list of institutions slated for appropriation. In the fall of 1948, Communist agitators exhorted those present at a mass student meeting at my university to occupy our dormitory and declare it a People's Dormitory (Népikollégium). I did not want to take part in the occupation and tried to leave the lecture hall. Guards at the doors would not let any attendees leave, believing they might alert the students at Szent Imre Kollégium, who would immediately protect their school by locking all the doors. I claimed to have an important appointment elsewhere and insisted that they allow me to leave. After some haggling, they let me go. However, they assigned a guard to escort me. Once on the street, we boarded a tram. I shook the man off by jumping from the tram when it slowed down. As soon as I saw that he was unable to follow me, I ran back to Szent Imre Kollégium and alerted everybody there about the plan to take over the dormitory.

But we could only delay the inevitable. The next day, the government converted the Szent Imre Kollégium into a People's Dormitory. A few days later, the new leadership expelled about a dozen students from the dorm. I was one of them. The following week's university newspaper described these events and mentioned me by name, describing me as

Mindszenthy's lackey (*Mindszenthy slepphordozója*). I was prepared for imprisonment or at least expulsion from the university. Surprisingly, nothing happened—at least not at that time.

Now, I had to find a place to live. I joined with three other expelled students and together we found an unoccupied apartment on the sixth floor of a building on Bartók Béla Road near Móricz Zsigmond Square. During weekdays, the living room was a photographic studio. The four of us got two bedrooms and full use of the kitchen and bathrooms. It was a good arrangement, and I stayed there for the next year and a half.

The day after Christmas 1948, the Communist secret police arrested Cardinal Mindszenty. He was tortured, and following a mock trial, he was sentenced to life imprisonment. Protests by Pope Pius XII, the United Nations, and many Western governments did not help. His life would change again during the 1956 revolution (see chapter fourteen).

By the end of 1948, the Communist Party had eliminated all opposition and achieved complete control of Hungary. The state owned all of the businesses. The press and radio became party propaganda organs. Qualified executives, even at the middle management level, were replaced with incompetent but loyal party members. All contact with capitalist imperialists, in other words, with all Western countries and institutions, ceased. Theaters showed only propaganda films made in Russia and the satellite countries. Western-made products disappeared from the shops. Meat, wheat, and most of what the country manufactured went to the Soviet Union. Food became scarce. Rations were introduced. Only pregnant women and those with babies could get milk. It became almost impossible to buy meat. And ÁVH (secret police) spies were everywhere. They listened to our words and reported anything suspicious or anticommunist. Nobody could be trusted anymore. The gates of large apartment houses had to be locked by ten o'clock at night, and concierges were required to report anyone receiving visitors after that hour. And because their job also included the collection and disposal of household garbage, concierges had to report anyone whose garbage too often contained bones, as this would indicate unauthorized income that made it possible to purchase meat at exorbitant black-market prices.

At the university, a handful of students who were loyal party members intimidated the students and faculty who did not belong to the party. A half hour before the first class, every student had to attend Szabad-Nép-Fél-Óra (Free People Half Hour). *Szabad Nép* (Free People) was the name of the party's newspaper. During Free People Half Hour, each of us had to talk about what we had read that day, how bad the capitalist imperialists were, and how Communism would triumph. The Russian language and the "science" of Marxism-Leninism became compulsory subjects not only at our university but at every university.

Following the ancient Roman principle of divide and conquer, Lenin's policy to control the peasant class called for allying with the poor, neutralizing middle-income farmers, and liquidating the wealthy peasant farmers, the so-called kulaks. Those who owned a farm larger than the arbitrarily set limit of about thirty acres were automatically classified as kulaks and had to give practically everything they produced to the state. If they kept anything beyond the minimum allotted for personal use, they were tortured, imprisoned, or sometimes executed, as an example to others. They were forbidden to sell their land, and the local police constantly harassed them.

Poor and middle-income peasants were forced into collective farms. Those who resisted were treated like the kulaks. Loyal party members, many without any agricultural experience, were put in charge of these farms. Collectivization ruined the once very productive Hungarian agricultural sector. The people, with the exception of the party elite, starved. Voters could, and were legally obligated to, vote only for candidates designated by the party. Of course, the Communists always won by 96 to 98 percent.

Back at the university, we had to attend long meetings and listen to endless speeches and lectures by uneducated party leaders. All of us had to stand up and applaud for minutes whenever the names of the national party head, Mátyás Rákosi, or Stalin (always preceded by the phrase, "our Father and our wise teacher, the great") were mentioned. Huge pictures of both men adorned nearly every office and were on display in all public places. At the edge of the Városliget, Budapest's most beautiful park, a Roman Catholic church was demolished and an enormous bronze statue of Stalin was erected in its place. (Years later, on October 23, 1956, our revolution would start with the toppling of this statue.)

On Stalin's and Rákosi's birthdays, all of us had to "voluntarily" offer to do extra work on weekends. Every year on May 1, we—that is, all factory and office workers, students, the armed forces, and the like—had to parade through the streets of Budapest and other cities carrying red flags or placards with a picture of Stalin or another Communist dignitary. We had to sing hymns glorifying "our wise leader" during these slow and tiring marches. Then, when we finally reached the end, we would pass in front of the Stalin statue, where top party officials, standing on a white marble platform under the statue, would review our parade.

Many of the projects proposed by inept party leaders were doomed to failure. Experts who tried to bring this to the leadership's attention were arrested and received long prison sentences for being saboteurs and imperialist agents.

And when these senseless projects failed, the blame fell on the engineers working on them. They then became the new group of saboteurs and imperialist agents, and they, too, were imprisoned. The draining of the Berek, a great swamp south of Lake Balaton, was Rákosi's pet project. Many great ancient and modern rulers, such as Julius Caesar and Mussolini, had drained swamps. Rákosi could not be left out of this illustrious company. The Zala River, the only major river flowing into Lake Balaton, passed through the Berek, which filtered its silt-laden waters. This prevented the sediment from reaching the lake, where it would spoil the water quality of central Europe's largest lake, a favorite vacation area for millions of Hungarians and other Europeans.

The Berek swamp was drained and the area was converted into agricultural land according to Rákosi's orders. The western end of Lake Balaton soon started to fill with silt. Several decades later, the swamps had to be restored to halt further silting and save the lake. The cost of restoring the Berek was many times higher than the cost of its draining.

A plan to grow orange and lemon trees was another one of Rákosi's expensive follies. Experts knew that because Hungary's winter temperatures frequently fall below zero, this project was doomed. But nobody dared to tell the dictator.

Derogatory statements or jokes about the Communist system or its leaders were punished by up to ten years of imprisonment. The jokes proliferated nevertheless. Telephones were bugged and letters were censored.

One day, Béla bácsi woke me early in the morning. He had just gotten word that the secret police had searched the homes of several colleagues. The most likely reason was to find some incriminating evidence to justify their arrest and the takeover of the bank by the Communist government. Béla bácsi knew that I had the military decorations of both my father and my uncle László, as well as my uncle's ceremonial sword. My uncle László Csicsery had died in 1919 fighting the Communists. Béla bácsi asked me to give him all of these items. He disposed of them all somewhere.

In the late spring of 1951, the government started the large-scale deportation of so-called class aliens and other unreliable elements from Budapest. All members of the former middle class who owned their homes, except doctors, engineers, and, of course, party members, were deported to villages in eastern Hungary. On alternating weekdays, between May 21 and July 18, a policeman rang the doorbell of the victims in the morning and, when admitted, read the order: "The Ministry of the Interior has designated a new home for you and your family. The head of the family may take 250 kilograms [about 550 pounds] of personal belongings, including bed, mattresses, and blankets. [Other family members were allowed less.] Be ready tomorrow morning! The government will take over your apartment and everything you leave in it." The next morning, the deportees were loaded onto trucks, taken to a railroad station, and transported to faraway places. The most unfortunate ended up in agricultural forced labor camps, or socalled social camps, which were surrounded by barbed wire and guarded by the secret police. The others were placed in kulak houses and had to work on farms. Workdays were twelve hours long, and the new arrivals were frequently required to walk long distances to reach the fields. They were not allowed to leave the villages to which they had been banished.

Tens of thousands were affected by these mass deportations, which were intended to rid the capital of unreliable class aliens who were agents of the capitalist imperialists. Bringing labor to the faltering collective farms was the second objective. And finally, the appropriated apartments were supposed to ease Budapest's housing shortage. The party elite and secret police officers soon occupied the better apartments. At the same time, the use of the word *deportation* was forbidden, and those who uttered it were severely punished. Zsuzsa Hantó's *Kitiltott Családok* (*Banished Families: Communist Repression of Class Enemies in Hungary*) describes the details of the deportations.[8]

When the sons of deportees came of military age, they were conscripted into forced labor camps. The same fate befell kulaks, ethnic Germans, and Serbians—these were the years of the Soviet-Yugoslav Split, when Stalin broke relations with Tito. Because my parents lived in the United States, and because I had attended a military school for almost two years, I was also an unreliable class alien, as I would discover in 1952 (see chapter six).

After Stalin's death in 1953, the more moderate government of Imre Nagy ended the deportations. Deportees could now move wherever they wanted, except to Budapest and five other large cities, and find work wherever they could. They never got their confiscated properties back, however.

Studying Amidst Chaos

WHEN I STARTED my final year at the university in September 1950, the apartment on Bartók Béla Road was no longer available, so I moved back to Béla bácsi's home. It was not easy to complete my studies during such tumultuous times, but somehow I survived until almost the end.

One morning an urgent call came from another uncle, Lehoczky Duci bácsi: he and his family had just received the order to pack. They asked me to come over right away and help move their most valuable furniture and other possessions to the homes of friends. I was planning to study all day for the next day's oral exam but helping them was more important. I spent the day carrying heavy furniture and large boxes to vehicles that took them to a safe place. The following day, I had to thank my guardian angel that the questions the examiner asked me were easy, and I was able to pass the exam.

Ex-owners of state-appropriated businesses, from large factories to corner grocery stores; lawyers; former landowners; bank executives; and retired officers of the Royal Hungarian Army were prime targets of the deportation. Gyula bácsi was a retired air force colonel. When one after another of his former friends was deported, he knew that sooner or later he too would be banished, so he made a preemptive move. He gave up his apartment on Mészáros Street; loaded all of his furniture and other possessions, including many books, onto a rented railroad car; and moved to a summer house in Balatonfenyves. A few of his friends and I helped him move. His plan worked: he escaped deportation. His new home, only a few hundred feet from Lake Balaton's shore, was fine in the summer but had to be upgraded to make it habitable during the long winter. Gyula bácsi and his wife, Ella néni, remained in Balatonfenyves for the rest of their lives. He eventually found work as a surveyor's helper. He passed away at the age of seventy-eight on June 17, 1973. A few years after that, Ella néni's brother, Király Bandi bácsi, who until that time had lived in Arad in Transylvania, moved in with her. She died on October 9, 1981.

About a month or so after I helped move Gyula bácsi, someone rang the bell at Béla bácsi's home early in the morning. It was a policeman—a member of the city police, not the secret police. Only Béla bácsi and I were at home. Margit néni and the children were in Balatonszemes. I overheard the discussion from the bathroom. The policeman read the names of Béla bácsi, Margit néni, and of all of their children except for Erzsike, who was not yet thirteen at the time. My name was also omitted. Béla bácsi asked the policeman what to do with the rest of his family, as they were not present. I remember the policeman whispering to him, "Leave them there; they will be better off where they are now than where we would take them." There were some decent people even among the police.

I worked with Béla bácsi and his friends all day, packing and transferring his more valuable furniture and other belongings to secure places. I had to gather all of my clothing and books and take them to the place of a friend who lived nearby. I also had to find a new home for myself. By late evening, someone had found me an empty apartment only a few blocks away. Szilárd Zemplén, a very nice retired lieutenant commander of the old Hungarian navy, owned the place. The next morning he told me that he had been an officer aboard the warship *Komárom* that was commanded by my uncle László Csicsery. He had been on the ship on June 26, 1919, when my uncle was shot and killed by the Communists. As this apartment was only a temporary refuge, I eventually rented a room next to the university from Mr. and Mrs. Jordán. Mr. Jordán's uncle, General János Jordán, had once been my father's superior. After I graduated, I rented a room on Margit Boulevard from Mrs. Medveczky, a childhood friend of my father's. The army had drafted her son for two years and his room was available. Mrs. Medveczky's apartment was a very good place to live.

I continued to prepare for my final examinations and took them during these chaotic months. Fortunately, I received excellent or good grades in all of the major subjects. In addition to the exams, we had to complete a thesis. My project was to determine the amount of the very mild laxative frangula emodin remaining in a waste fraction. If the amount was significant, I was to devise a way to recover it. The minor problem was that hardly any frangula emodin was left in that particular fraction. The major problem was that I had to help relatives pack and move their valuables and, later, move myself during the short time assigned for my thesis work. A junior member of the teaching staff supervised each thesis. My mentor was the future Nobel laureate George Oláh (1927–2017). He understood my predicament and helped me complete the thesis. This was the beginning of our friendship.

During the school year, I had neglected our most important subject, Marxism-Leninism. I did not read the required writings of Lenin and Stalin or articles in the party newspaper. I even skipped some of the classes. Now I did not have enough time to prepare for the oral test. But lack of knowledge was not my undoing. The first question the examiner asked me was about the Social Democrats. To better consolidate their power, the Communists had forced the Social Democrats into an uneasy alliance named the Hungarian Workers' Party. However, the day before my exam, I heard on the forbidden BBC or Voice of America radio news that the secret police had arrested several leading Social Democrats. Knowing this, I answered, "They were agents of the fascists and capitalist imperialists, but now they've finally received their just punishment." The examiner's face suddenly changed, and he asked me, "Where did you hear this?" I immediately realized that I had made a horrible mistake. The party had not yet announced these arrests, and the only way of knowing about them was from forbidden foreign radio broadcasts. There were no further questions. I failed the test.

During the next two weeks I read nothing but works by Lenin and Stalin. Lenin's works were clear and logical, but Stalin's writings were hard to understand because he wrote in a circuitous and complicated way. When I thought I knew enough, I took the exam and I passed with a satisfactory grade, one step better than failing. It was good enough for me.

A few days before this exam, a friend told me to look at something in the central hall of the university's main building. A large poster at the very center of hall proclaimed, "The Shame of Our University: Zsigmond Csicsery, who received As in all of his subjects but flunked Marxism-Leninism." Only one other student's name was on this list. He was the architectural engineering student László Papp, who was expelled from the university just before graduation. László Papp had been a schoolmate of mine at military school, the best in our class. In 1945, we had been together in Germany and had slept in the same hole in the ground at the Bad Kreuznach prisoner-of-war camp. After 1956, he left Hungary for the United States where he became a very famous and successful architect. We still correspond with each other.

After my second year of university, our chemical engineering class had been split into three equal groups: inorganic chemistry, organic chemistry, and agricultural-plus-food chemistry. I had chosen the organic chemistry group. After my third year, I had spent the summer as a student worker at the Kőbányai Gyógyszerárugyár research laboratory. The company had previously been called the Richter Gedeon Gyógyszergyár, a pharmaceutical factory. I liked working there and made many friends. I looked forward to continuing there following graduation.

By the time our class graduated, most of my classmates had also gotten jobs. Then one day all of us received official letters assigning our future workplaces. For some inexplicable reason, all organic chemical engineers were sent to inorganic workplaces and vice versa. My future place was to be in an obscure sulfuric acid plant. When I complained, the only thing I could do was to select another inorganic workplace. There was no appeal. I chose the Forte Photochemical factory in Vác, a small city twenty-five miles (42 km) north of Budapest. Forte had been a Kodak factory prior to the war, and after the war, Kodak did not repossess it. The plant's workers took over the plant and very successfully restarted it. During my interview at Forte, I realized that the factory was a pleasant place, my work would involve interesting organic chemistry, and my future coworkers would be decent people. I applied for the job and my application was accepted. I was to start in late summer.

A few weeks later I was summoned to party headquarters. After a thorough search at the gate, an armed secret policeman led me to one of the offices. Because I had failed Marxism-Leninism, the school's most important subject, making me the "shame of the university," I feared the worst. But I had been summoned for a completely different reason. An important-looking party functionary informed me that the relevant ministry had mixed up our job assignments by mistake and now our magnanimous party was ready to rectify the situation. Not wanting to accept anything from the party, I told him not to change anything and that I would be happy working at the Forte factory. I later learned that new choices were offered to all of that year's graduates.

CHAPTER FIVE

Working at Forte in Vác (1951–52)

LIFE IN HUNGARY had become increasingly difficult by 1951. Food production had fallen because forced collectivization had destroyed the nation's agriculture. The Russians took the bulk of whatever little was produced. Rarely could common workers find any meat, butter, or other dairy products, so they were almost always hungry. People ate lunch on workdays at workplace cafeterias. The usual meal was a weak soup and some type of potato, cabbage, or bean dish. Meat was served only once a week, and to irritate Roman Catholics (about two-thirds of the population), who had to abstain from eating meat on Fridays, "meat day" was always Friday. The Council of Bishops responded to this by canceling all fast days except Good Friday and Ash Wednesday. Stores were empty except for bookstores, which were stocked almost exclusively with the works of Lenin and Stalin and other Russian propaganda publications. It became impossible to find good-quality clothing or footwear, even if you had money. To boost sagging production, workers were forced to work "voluntary" overtime on many weekends. In contrast, the party elite and members of the secret police continued to obtain whatever they wanted despite constant shortages and thus lived well.

As the economy went downhill, government terror intensified. The Communists arrested, convicted, and imprisoned on trumped-up charges thousands of men and women who stood in their way. An unknown number of people simply disappeared into internment camps without trial. In the spring of 1950, the secret police set up at least four such secret camps. The camp near Recsk was the most infamous and the cruelest in the Hungarian Gulag system.[9, 10] Other camps were established in Kistarcsa, Tiszalök, and Kazincbarcika, all locations in northeastern Hungary. Interned detainees worked under inhuman conditions in unsafe coal mines or stone quarries. Unlike convicted prisoners, these detainees had absolutely no way to communicate with their families or lawyers—not that any lawyer dared to help anybody in those years.

Even top party leaders were not immune from the terror. Infighting between dictator Rákosi and his clique—all of whom spent the years before 1945 in Moscow—and Minister of Interior László Rajk had culminated in Rajk's spectacular show trial and hanging in 1949. Many others associated with Rajk were also executed. The execution or imprisonment of less-important enemies was not publicized.

I started my work in Vác under these brutal conditions. I realized very soon that few true Communists could be counted among the workers, and most party members were openly critical of the Communist system and the Russian occupation. In those days, high-level positions at most companies required party membership. Some people compromised and joined the party; others gave up on any chance for career advancement and suffered the consequences.

The Commute to Vác

A LOVELY CITY on the eastern bank of the Danube, Vác was also home to an infamous prison—the community's largest institution—filled with political prisoners. Other than its nineteenth-century cathedral, the bishop's residence, and an arch of triumph built for the visit of Empress Maria Theresa in 1764, the city had few noteworthy buildings. It was a quiet, provincial place, largely untouched by progress.

My work in Vác was interesting, as I learned much about the chemistry of photography. But the housing shortage in the city was even worse than in Budapest, so I had to commute twenty-six miles (42 km) each way on Hungary's oldest railroad line, which dated to 1846. In the past, the train had made the trip in fifty-six minutes, and because the Forte factory had its own station about two miles (3.5 km) south of the main Vác station, the time was even shorter. The trip now required seventy minutes. Some progress! A few dozen other people also commuted to the Forte plant from Budapest. We had to leave Budapest's Western Terminal on the 5:50 a.m. train to be able to start work at 7:00 a.m. But that workers' train was almost always behind schedule. Fortunately, we were never reprimanded for being late. The tram or bus ride from my home to the Western Terminal took about twenty minutes, and because trams and buses were always overcrowded, I sometimes could not board at all. If I missed the 5:50 a.m. train, I could catch another one a half hour later, but then I was really late for work!

The workers' train consisted of old boxcars originally built for cattle. They were very hot in summer and very cold in winter. Each car had only a few wooden benches, which meant many people had to stand for the entire trip. There were no stairs, so getting in or out of the car wasn't easy, either. Even reading was difficult during the long rides, as the cars were shaky and poorly lit. Such uncomfortable travel was a nuisance. Six days a week I had to get up before 5:00 a.m. and did not get back home until 6:00 p.m. I remember being tired and sleepy most of the time. Other than a few concerts and operas, I had little entertainment and not much social life.

The Forte Challenge

FILM AND PAPER are made by coating cellulose acetate film or high-quality paper with a gelatin emulsion in which silver chloride is suspended. Photosensitivity and resolution depend on the size of the silver chloride crystals and are inversely related to each other. Thus, high-sensitivity film (that is, one with a high ASA rating) is always grainier than a less sensitive one. The sensitivity of freshly prepared film decreases as the film ages. As photographers do not like to cope with unknown sensitivities, stabilizers are added to the emulsion to slow down deterioration. The stabilizers employed in the past worked at the expense of sensitivity, which meant the stabilized film was as sensitive as it would have been after a year or two on the shelf. Then a German company invented a stabilizer that did not decrease sensitivity, and Forte was able to purchase it from the Germans at a very reasonable price. However, starting in late 1951, the Germans began selling it only premixed with gelatin, which made the product prohibitively expensive. Forte either had to do something to remain competitive or go out of business. The company director announced that he would make whoever solved this problem a Stakhanovite, named for a prodigiously productive Soviet miner named Stakhanov. Winning this honor was the Communist equivalent of something like an Oscar in the United States. Stakhanovism represented an attempt to maximize output by competitive record breaking among workers.[11]

Several of us chemical engineers and chemists immediately started to work on the problem. We soon found that the stabilizer was a 7:3 mixture of salicylic acid and an unknown white crystalline substance. I succeeded in separating and purifying enough of this unknown material to measure its composition and molecular weight. But knowing the composition of an organic compound is only the beginning of its identification. Forte's laboratory and analytical facilities were limited, so I received permission to continue my investigation in Budapest. That meant no more getting up at five o'clock in the morning and no more long commutes for a while. I had access to the library at Technical University, and friends at the university performed spectroscopic and other physical measurements on my material. Other friends at the Kőbányai Gyógyszerárugyár, where I had worked one summer as a student, permitted me to work in their well-equipped research laboratory.

I soon narrowed down the possibilities to three. The next step was to synthesize each one to find out which of them, if any, was the stabilizer. One of the three was a rather complicated cyclic molecule. Its five-member ring consisted of four nitrogen atoms and only one carbon. I started with this one. Its synthesis took about two weeks. During the last two days, I worked nonstop. I did not even go home to sleep. When I filtered the final product, I could not believe my nose: it smelled exactly like our stabilizer. I collected the few grams I had made and took the first train to Vác. Arriving at midday, I put the small jar on my supervisor's desk and said nothing. She jumped, "Is this 'it'? Is it really it?" And then she phoned the director and the other senior engineers. Everybody was happy. I became the hero of Forte. I went home and slept for two days.

The next week I returned to Kőbányai Gyógyszerárugyár for a few more weeks and developed a manufacturing process for the new stabilizer. Forte had neither the facilities nor the experience to perform such syntheses. I contracted with

Kőbányai Gyógyszerárugyár to produce the stabilizer for Forte at a reasonable price. My work was completed.

At about this time, a wonderful opportunity arose: a new job at a prestigious research institute. A chemical university and two chemical research institutes had recently been established in Veszprém, a beautiful city not far from Lake Balaton. Construction of the new buildings had been completed, and the three new institutions had started recruiting. They were looking for recent graduates. A dozen of my former classmates were already working there. My superiors at Forte gave me the best possible recommendations and wished me good luck.

However, "class-aliens" like myself could not work at universities because "the People's Democracy cannot allow capitalist imperialists to educate future generations of scientists!" Instead, I had to apply at the NEVIKI (Nehéz Vegyipari Kutató Intézet, or Heavy Chemical Research Institute). My application was accepted, and I moved to Veszprém. Housing construction for the new research staff was way behind schedule, and I ended up living in the institute's cafeteria building. For two weeks, I and other new staff did nothing but help the professional movers carry heavy boxes full of laboratory equipment, chemicals, furniture, and books. The move was just about complete when I received a registered letter. It was a draft notice, but not from the army. I was being drafted into forced labor. And there was no appeal.

CHAPTER SIX

Forced Labor (1952–53)

AFTER A LONG ride in crowded boxcars, about five hundred other draftees and I arrived at Miskolc, a large industrial city in northeastern Hungary. We marched to a construction site beyond the northern suburbs, where we were billeted in newly built military barracks. We were treated like prisoners, with armed sentries guarding us, and were issued old military uniforms that had been discarded by the regular army after they adopted Russian-style uniforms. Although we were considered unworthy to serve in the army, discipline followed army regulations. I later learned that the total number of forced laborers in the country at that time was between twelve and sixteen thousand.[12]

Just before I was drafted for forced labor, I had read the works of the Stoic philosopher Epictetus. Born a slave circa AD 55, Epictetus believed that all external events are beyond our control. We can only control our own actions. Therefore, we should accept whatever happens calmly. Trying to control what is uncontrollable results in suffering. His philosophy helped me to preserve my optimism during my years of forced labor, imprisonment, and torture.

Our first task was to make our own bedding by stuffing straw into a sack. For somebody who had never stuffed a straw sack in his life, this was surprisingly difficult and quite exhausting. We used the freshly made sacks on the bunk beds on which we slept.

We received only half portions of regular military rations. It was not much, but it was nutritious and nearly adequate. Many of my fellow draftees told me that the rations were better than what they had been eating before they arrived, and they were certainly more than what I had been able to afford as a beginning chemical engineer.

I was assigned to the third company of a four-company battalion. Each company occupied a separate floor of the barracks, and with few exceptions, the officers and guards were from the bottom of the officers' list. Some were alcoholics, others had spent time in prison, and most of them were incompetent and unintelligent. They treated us like dirt. Our company was lucky because our commander, Lieutenant Váradi, was an exception. He was soft-spoken, well educated, intelligent, and had a good sense of humor. Most important, he was very decent, and as far as I know, treated us as well as circumstances allowed. His actions made me wonder why he had to serve as an officer of unreliables and enemies of the people and where his sympathies really lay.

The secret police officer assigned to our battalion had his office and living quarters on our floor. His name was Somosváry or Somosvári—most likely not his real name. The officers supervising us feared him more than we did. After all, as forced laborers we felt that we did not have much more to lose. But we should have known better.

In the summer of 1952, the government drafted men born in 1929, 1930, and 1931 for the labor camp. The majority were sons of kulaks. Swabians (or Svábs, an ethnic German minority in Hungary) constituted another large group. They and the kulak children were hardworking, decent, and honest. There were also criminals who had spent time in prison for stealing or robbing. Our company even included a murderer. Only a few of us were from the middle or upper classes. These included two other chemical engineers, one of whom was a former classmate. At school, he was, or pretended to be, a devout Communist. He was drafted because his father was a Serbian Orthodox priest. When Stalin broke relations with Tito, Hungary's Serbian and Croatian minorities became "unreliable." Later at the Várpalota prison coal mine, I worked with his older brother, who was not a Communist. He thought his brother deserved his fate and hoped that the experience would bring him to his senses. Three decades later, I met my former classmate again. He had become a professor at the Technical University of Budapest.

At the beginning, a few Jehovah's Witnesses were also drafted into forced labor because they refused to serve in the army. We wore old army uniforms, so they considered forced labor a form of military service and refused to do anything, especially the construction work that involved building barracks for the army. They would not even participate in compulsory morning calisthenics. The officers tried to compromise, transferring them to kitchen duty. But they even refused to work there. Eventually, the military police arrested them. After being convicted, a few of them were placed in a prison work camp not far from our site. Their job at the new site was to build the same barracks. Because they were now prisoners, they considered themselves martyrs and worked very hard—much harder than other prisoners. I never understood their logic.

The army contracted with civilian construction companies to build barracks and other facilities. Although run by civilians, these companies were also state owned. The contractors had their own architects and masons, electricians and plumbers but no unskilled workers. The army provided forced laborers, in other words, us, as the unskilled workforce. The accounting was complicated: the army paid the contractors, and the contractors paid the army for our work.

Every worker in the Communist system had a daily "norm," that is, the amount of work that must be completed during eight hours. These norms were set at almost unattainably high levels. Anyone working less than 100 percent was reprimanded or punished. Those who surpassed 100 percent were rewarded with privileges. Forced laborers worked under the same system. The privileges we received were passes to the city of Miskolc on Sunday afternoons or perhaps even a few days leave to visit our families. Our guards were also rewarded when the company performed well.

Each morning, our guards marched us to a construction site. Every couple of days or so, a foreman or an architect outlined the tasks for the next few days. Most of us had to shovel something or push wheelbarrows loaded with bricks, sand, or cement. Our performance was very poor at the beginning. No matter how hard we exerted ourselves, we were unused to this type of work and never got beyond 40 to 50 percent of the norm. And yet we were dead tired when we got back to our quarters.

As we began to learn our new trades, our performance improved, but we still performed way below 100 percent. We soon discovered that our officers had no mathematical skills, and that most of them were incapable of learning accounting. They selected a handful of us who had the necessary experience to do the accounting and calculate the norms. It became obvious that none of the officers would ever notice misplaced decimal points. From then on, our performance was always a few points above 100 percent.

Fixing paperwork was easy, but our daily results also had to look better than what we actually accomplished. Sometimes this was easy, sometimes not. Newly constructed walls look darker than the previous day's work because they are still wet. Soon we realized that it was much easier to pour some water on what we had completed the day before than to work very hard building more new walls. The amount of bricks, sand, cement, and the like transported from a distant warehouse or rail terminal to the construction site was determined by counting the number of round trips the truck made during the workday. Many more round trips could be made with much less work if only a small fraction of the bricks or other material was unloaded at the construction site. The civilian truck drivers cooperated in these scams because they were paid according to the number of round trips completed.

Every morning, we started working furiously under the watchful eyes of our guards. After an hour or two, the guards would get bored and disappear. Our work slowed down or sometimes completely stopped until lunchtime, when the guards would then reappear. The afternoons were similar.

By late fall, all of these tricks had made life much easier, plus we were rewarded. Family members could come to visit us, and every once in a while, we were allowed short leaves. But all this did not obscure the reality that we were forced laborers with uncertain futures. We had no idea how long we would remain slaves. We suspected that our present condition would continue for the time being, but if the cold war turned hot, we would most likely be exterminated.

Our officers knew why each one of us was there. They knew that for two years I had been in a military school under the old regime. Consequently, they appointed me the ügyeletes (orderly). I was required to make a daily report on how many of the company of 135 were ready to work and how many were sick or away for some other reason. As an orderly, I was also responsible for the cleanliness of the company's quarters, including bathrooms and hallways, and for leading the company to meals. Finally, for twenty-four hours, either I or one of my two helpers had to stand guard. Against whom? And how? With a shovel? It was a demanding job that required full attention, but it was far better than carrying huge sacks of cement. I was also able to read and study during the long hours at the guard table. Of course, being in charge of maintaining order and cleanliness did not make me many friends.

The officers gave us pep talks, which was probably a difficult task for the less educated among them. Several asked me secretly to ghostwrite their speeches. So-called political officers assigned to every company were supposed to ensure that all of us became good Communists. Our company's political officer, Sublieutenant Kitler, was an uneducated and unintelligent man. When his turn came to give a lecture, he, too, asked me to write it. I inserted many difficult-to-pronounce non-Hungarian words into his speech, including the word *monarhia* (monarchy). His speech was a disaster. All of us, even the officers present, laughed as he struggled through his lecture. He pronounced *monarhia* each time as "mamarcia." This earned him the nickname Mamarcia, even among some officers. A few weeks later, he was discharged from the army. I don't know how much the lecture I wrote contributed to his downfall; I would feel badly if it did. Although he was not intelligent, he was not a bad person. He never hurt us.

As our performance—at least on paper—regularly exceeded the 100 percent norm, we were rewarded with passes. Sometimes we could go home for a few days, so I went to Budapest several times. On each visit, I would ask friends at the university to intervene on my behalf to help secure an early release so I could go back to work. Some of them tried, or at least they told me they had tried, but nothing helped. These were difficult times, indeed. Every day the party exhorted the population to intensify the fight against all reactionary forces and class enemies.

Early that summer, tragedy struck my uncle Béla bácsi and his family. His father was dying in Balatonszemes, and Béla bácsi received permission to leave the farm to which he had been deported in order to make a last visit to his father. He overstayed his leave, so the police arrested him, along with Margit néni and the children. They shipped them to the farm in Kardoskút, the place where they were to have gone the year before. Around the same time, the authorities suddenly confiscated their villa and the two other villas my uncles and aunts and our family spent every summer at Balatonszemes. Until this point, my grandmother had owned these villas and the adjoining orchard. The party handed our property to the Soviet-Hungarian Friendship Association, and the association proceeded to cut down all the fruit trees and build a large resort for party members. When Communist rule in Hungary ended in 1989, some former owners got their confiscated property back. For some reason, these villas were not returned to our family.

I used one of my passes to visit Béla bácsi and Margit néni in Kardoskút. Duci bácsi, another of my uncles, and his family had been deported to another village. The adults and older children had to work in the fields, but they were healthy and had enough to eat. Both families had become good friends with the kulak farmers with whom they were forced to live.

During my stay in Kardoskút, one of the kulak farmers woke me early one morning and asked me to help him. One of his cows was having a difficult delivery. The two of us had to pull the calf by its legs, and we had to hurry to prevent the newborn from suffocating. We struggled for several hours and were both completely covered with blood. But the calf was delivered alive. The farmer was very happy and grateful. He named the calf Zsiga in my honor.

Back in Miskolc, one of the forced laborers, a man called Horváth, did not return in time from his weekend pass. This was a serious matter. Being AWOL earned a long prison sentence. My duty as orderly required that I report his absence as soon as I became aware of it. I was hoping that he would show up by evening and kept my mouth shut. That night I made his bunk bed look occupied and hoped that he would be there by morning. He was not. I decided to wait another day. And then I waited one more day. Finally, on the fourth morning, he showed up, prepared for the worst. I told him that none of the officers knew he was AWOL and that he should act as if he had been back all the time. He was very grateful. We met again later in a prison coal mine.

At the Diósgyőr Steel Mill

THAT FALL, A group of freshly graduated officers was assigned to our units. They looked like the bottom of their class. One of them hated me because, in his eyes, I represented the reactionary imperialist forces. He promptly relieved me of my assignment as orderly. I didn't care, as just about this same time, our company was transferred to Diósgyőr to work in the steel mill.

The Diosgyor smelters and steel mills were the second largest in Hungary. The Communists emphasized heavy industry, especially steel and iron, and built new or expanded existing smelters and Martin furnaces. The problem was that Hungary had neither iron ore nor good-quality coal. The country had to import low-quality ore from the Soviet Union at a very high price. The steel produced was sold to the Soviets at an artificially low price. The result was that the more the steel mill turned out the more money it lost.

At Diósgyőr, we were housed in single-floor wooden barracks. Every morning the guards handed us over to an engineer or foreman from the mill, who assigned our daily tasks. Usually we had to shovel slag into wheelbarrows and take it somewhere. The weather had turned cold, and it rained or snowed frequently. Our guards usually disappeared soon after we started working. As we shoveled the slag, we had to leave a one-square-foot-diameter column untouched. The engineers calculated our daily accomplishment by measuring the height of this column, called *baba,* or "puppet." When nobody was watching, we built the column higher instead of shoveling and then sat around a makeshift fire talking and telling jokes. I preferred to learn something about steelmaking, and as soon as I could, I slipped away to see the mills. Communist propaganda has always maintained that steelworkers are the best and most faithful members of the party. That made me worry that they would recognize my forced laborer status from my uniform, and I would get into trouble. Exactly the opposite happened.

By 1952, almost everyone in Hungary hated the Communist system. Even most of those who had at the beginning believed in the promised blessings of Socialism and Communism were now disillusioned. The system was held together by secret police terror and the occupying Russian forces. As the steelworkers recognized my status, all of them became very friendly and told me about their work and lives. Most had cousins or nephews in forced labor or in prison. One of them directed me to an engineer. When I told him that I was a chemical engineer, he treated me like a colleague, showing me the blast furnace and explaining its operation. Then he took me to the main library and asked for a library card for me so I could take books with me and learn more about metallurgy. He told me to come back the next day. I did, and we went to see the Martin furnaces and the steel presses that made rods and sheet metal from red-hot ingots. Everything I saw that day I found highly interesting.

After one of my daily tours, I told my colleagues how foolish it was for them to bring us unreliables to work in this important industrial establishment where we would have the opportunity to do some real damage, such as blowing up a blast furnace. I did not know that a secret police informer was in my audience. This would lead to serious difficulties down the road.

Although it made little sense to manufacture iron in a country that lacked both iron ore and black coal (Hungary had only low-quality brown coal deposits), this blast furnace was the pride of the Communists. Low-quality iron ore was shipped from the Ukraine, and coal came from Poland in flatcars. The railroad yard where these trains were waiting to be unloaded was behind our barracks. Armed soldiers guarded the coal day and night to prevent theft. The people of Miskolc and Diósgyőr and of every other place in Hungary had almost no fuel to heat their homes. So every evening at nightfall, long lines of people carrying backpacks, baskets, or some other bag appeared seemingly from nowhere at the rail yards. They came to steal coal. Instead of preventing the theft, the soldiers looked the other way. Some even helped the women and the elderly fill their bags. Our barracks had a little iron stove, but we were never issued any fuel. Along with the others, we got our coal from the rail yard. But I found our barracks always so overheated at night that I never slept well.

Then one day the order came: György Schey, Tamás Major, László Doleschál, János Tuschák, Miklós Miletics, Tamás Szemere, two others, and I were transferred to Budapest. The nine of us were to take the next train, and after arrival in Budapest, we were to go immediately to another forced labor battalion. There we would receive further orders.

CHAPTER SEVEN

Back in Budapest (1953)

OF THE NINE forced laborers transferred to Budapest, six of us were from Budapest and two others had friends or relatives in the city. On arrival, we quickly agreed that we should all first go home, then meet again in two days and report together at the address we had been given. And so it happened. But the clerk at the forced labor battalion we reported to had no idea why we were there and what he should do with us, so he asked us to return the next day. We agreed and left to enjoy another free day. After sending us away four or five more times, the clerk finally learned that we had been assigned to a different forced labor unit. He gave us the address, and we went there the next morning. Although the people in charge there did not send us home, they also had no idea what to do with us. We were assigned living quarters but given no work orders for a week. That suited us fine.

One day around noon, the nine of us were resting in the courtyard when a jeep entered and an officer jumped out and asked if any of us could draw. I volunteered at once. He ordered me into the jeep, filled out some forms at the unit's office, and took me to a small building not far from the artillery barracks where my family had lived from 1932 to 1939. I joined three other forced laborers at the little house. The officer explained that he had to put together an exhibition on how to care for army property properly and avoid waste. We were to prepare dozens of large posters to illustrate his points. Our workroom would also serve as our living quarters. The complex accommodated about thirty other forced laborers and housed some military offices. We would receive our meals there, as well. He asked us to make a list of the drawing supplies we needed.

The four of us soon became good friends. We recognized that with this assignment we had hit the jackpot. Instead of construction work, we had a comfortable office, easy and enjoyable work, much better food, and real beds. The beds posed one problem, however: there were only three of them. Because my three roommates were from families who lived far from Budapest and they had no close acquaintances in the city, they had to sleep at this place. So I took the opportunity to benefit from my numerous relatives and friends around town. Our compound was unguarded. On evenings when I was not already downtown on some business, I slipped out and went to sleep at the home of a relative or friend. Each morning I had to draw my daily provisions, which were the same each day: some bread, a tin can of meat, and one hundred grams (four ounces) of fine butter. Meat and butter were very scarce in those days, available only to the party elite, members of the secret police, and some army units. With my daily ration, I could compensate family and friends who offered me a place to sleep.

One of my new colleagues was Papp, a former air force cadet. One day Papp and one of his flying instructors had tried to fly from Hungary to Austria. Fighter planes forced them down, and the secret police tortured both of them. The officer knew that nothing could save him. However, to save Papp, he steadfastly maintained that Papp did not know anything about his escape plan. The officer was hanged and Papp was sent to forced labor. He left Hungary after the 1956 revolution and eventually got an engineering degree. For a while he lived in Marin County, north of San Francisco. I was also living in the Bay Area then and we got together a few times to talk about the bad old days.

A silent Swabian boy was my second new colleague. The third roommate was named Záhonyi. A great artist, he was probably the best and most imaginative in the group. He had been a secret-police border guard, serving near the Yugoslav border, and he had shot a man. The man did not die right away, and Záhonyi's superiors were able to interrogate him. Apparently, the man had some legitimate business near the border, and Záhonyi had shot him by mistake, which meant he had to be punished, so he was transferred to forced labor. Záhonyi was a great storyteller. In civilian life, he had worked on a stud farm, assisting the stallions to mount the mares. I didn't know that stallions need a man's guiding hand for the most natural act of life. Záhonyi was the only man I met in Hungary who truly and sincerely believed in the ideals of Communism.

• • •

WHO WERE THE Communists? What were their backgrounds and why did they join the party? Based on my personal experience and on discussions with others, I believe that most members of the Communist Party came from one of the following groups.

1. The dictator and perhaps a dozen top lieutenants were veteran leaders of Hungary's brief Communist regime in 1919. Many had spent at least part of the interwar years in Moscow and were trained there. According to rumor, most were Soviet citizens. Mátyás Rákosi, the dictator, and Ernő Gerő, one of Rákosi's right-hand men and later secretary of the Communist Party, were members of Communist

International, or Comintern, the highest Communist executive group.

2. Officers of the secret police and other sadists.

3. After the Russians defeated the Germans, people who had been persecuted by the Nazis were grateful to the Russians for saving their lives and giving back their freedom. Some felt obligated to join the party. Others joined for the opportunity to take vengeance on their real or imagined persecutors.

4. Turncoats. Many low-level members of the Arrow Cross Party (Hungarian Nazis) joined the Communist Party to cover their pasts and avoid punishment.

5. The Communist Party forced the Social Democratic Party to unite with them. Any leaders who resisted were arrested and imprisoned. The others automatically became members of the enlarged Communist Party, now renamed the Magyar Dolgozók Pártja (Hungarian Workers' Party). It was difficult and dangerous to renounce party membership.

6. Soon after the war, the new government subdivided the large estates owned by the aristocracy, the Catholic Church, and other big landholders. The party took advantage of the fact that most of the people who benefited from land reform were uneducated and gullible and could therefore be easily brainwashed. The party told them that the aristocracy and other rich landowners had caused their poverty and misery and that the Communist Party was responsible for the land reform. Some previously landless peasants felt obligated to join the party. A few years later, the Communists forced them to give up their newly acquired lands and join communes.

7. Many mid- and higher-level executives, engineers, other professionals, and people in city, county, and other administrative positions either had to join the party or lose their

jobs. Some of them joined the party. Others maintained, perhaps correctly, that staying in their jobs would allow them to help people. The reasoning went something like this: it would be much better for everybody if I make the decisions, rather than some cruel and/or incompetent Communist!

8. Opportunists used party membership to advance their careers, for material gain, and in many cases to exact revenge for real or imagined past injustices. Many former bosses were denounced and suffered prison sentences for disciplining or firing an incompetent subordinate who later became a party functionary.

9. Stories circulated that some petty criminals avoided serving time in prison by becoming members of the secret police and the party.

10. The desire to redistribute wealth, to eliminate differences between rich and poor, and to correct the mistakes of the capitalist system led many to embrace the ideas of Socialism. Curiously, most of these were not landless peasants or members of the oppressed proletariat. They were leftist intellectuals, often attracted by Lenin's clear and logical writings. Lenin called them "useful idiots." In the beginning, these naïve people believed in a utopia. But most of them soon realized that Communist practice differs greatly from theory, that the Hungarian Communist Party blindly followed the Kremlin's orders, and that the first objective of Communism in Hungary was to incorporate the country into Stalin's empire.

Party members did not have easy lives. They were required to attend countless meetings and take part in seminars at which they were brainwashed. They had to read the works of Stalin and Lenin and the party's daily newspaper. They were not allowed to go to church or to have their children baptized.

Somehow most of them managed to do the latter secretly. The rules also required them to work hard, lead an exemplary moral and honest life, and remain incorruptible. In practice, most were incompetent and lazy, immoral and dishonest, and open to bribes.

•   •   •

WHEN I VOLUNTEERED as a draftsman, I thought the officer was talking about engineering drawing. My roommates were excellent artists; I was not. I spent my drafting career sharpening pencils, drawing frames, and writing any engineering-type letters that were required.

Our officer treated us well. At first he drove me to downtown Budapest to help purchase the supplies. Later, whenever we needed something, he filled out a day pass and let me go out into the city alone.

The other thirty forced laborers at our compound had a curious job. The colonel in charge of the army's coal and other fuels noticed that much of the poor-quality coal disintegrated during transport and was wasted. At that time, old-fashioned cast-iron stoves heated most army barracks. These could not burn powdered coal. His idea was to compress the powder into briquettes using acid sludge as the binder. In those days, petroleum refineries removed basic nitrogen compounds from crude oil with concentrated sulfuric acid. The resulting corrosive, stinky, viscous liquid product was called acid sludge. The colonel developed a process that cemented the coal powder with this sludge, but the sludge had to be neutralized to eliminate corrosion. He needed a chemist to supervise the neutralization and selected me. We had met previously and had discovered that, as a young officer in the prewar army, he had known my father. He treated me like a nephew instead of a disposable slave.

As our posters neared completion, the thought of returning to our regular units depressed all four of us. This new assignment seemed like a good way for me to postpone that unpleasant reality, and I worked hard to do my best. Finally, I could work as a chemist! I spent days at the university library reading everything I could find on acid sludge. My job was to calculate the amount of lime needed for the neutralization.

Then one day the order came: report at once to your battalion. This applied to the nine of us from Diósgyőr. I ran to the colonel's office. He looked at the order and immediately called the general in charge of all forced labor units. He told him that he needed my expertise in his very important project. He waited for a while for the answer. Then I saw his face turn pale as he asked, "Who can order you?" The general must have told him something because after he hung up the telephone, he turned to me and asked, "What have you done? What could you have done?" He did not wait for my answer. Instead, he told me that there was nothing further he could do for me. I should do as ordered. He added that he would try his best to save me.

The next morning, I joined the others, and we worked together in construction for a few days. But now we were down to eight. They told me that two weeks earlier a military vehicle had picked up György Schey. They had not seen him since.

Election day was a week away and our officers gave us one propaganda talk after another in the run-up. We had to pledge that we would vote for the Communist Party and not take the option of voting secretly. It was a circus. The result was predictable: the Communists received about 98 percent of the vote. Our reward was a weekend furlough.

CHAPTER EIGHT

Arrest and Imprisonment by the Secret Police (1953)

THE MORNING WE returned to our battalion following our furlough, four of us, including Tamás Major, were arrested and taken to an empty cellar below an innocent-looking house near Váci Road. We spent the next two weeks there. The sole object in the cellar was a bullet-riddled paper target hanging on the wall.

We slept on the floor with no blankets. We had to rise at daybreak and stand in the corner of the cell facing the wall until dark. The only way to judge the passage of time was by watching the ray of sunlight, emitted from the miniature window behind us, traverse the wall. An armed guard was stationed outside the door. If he heard any noise, he opened the door and reminded us that we were not supposed to move. We were able to whisper to one another, but because we suspected that the room was bugged, we avoided saying anything that could be used against us. We passed the time swapping old jokes. Our only meal was a little watery soup at noon.

Every day our captors led us, one at a time, upstairs for interrogation and beating. If I had any doubt where we were, it was dispelled when I saw the picture of Felix Dzerzhinsky, founder of Cheka, the Soviet secret police. (Cheka was later renamed GPU, then NKVD.) Beneath Dzerzhinsky's picture was a quote: "What you would not tell your enemy, don't tell your friends!"

Usually one of the two or three secret police officers present started these interrogations with an order to confess. When I said that I had nothing to confess, he would respond that I knew my crimes well and should start my confession. I was never told what my crimes were. Then the officers would start torturing me. Most often I had to "drill a well," that is, put my index finger on the ground and walk around it in circles continuously. One of the officers would then start beating me with a heavy leather belt until I bled or got dizzy from walking in circles and collapsed. One day the belt buckle hit my nose. It started to bleed and a drop fell on the officer's uniform. He immediately stopped torturing me and ordered the guard to lead me back to the cellar. From then on, I always pointed my nose in the direction from which the belt came. If my nose started bleeding, I shook my head so that my blood would stain my tormentor's pants. That usually ended the torture.

Three of us were always covered with blood each time we were brought back to the cellar. But not Tamás Major. One time we asked him how he avoided bleeding. He said he always bled so heavily that they cleaned him up before bringing him back. Unfortunately, we were naïve and believed him. We later learned that he was an informer who had been planted among the forced laborers of the Miskolc battalion to report on suspicious conversations. After his arrest, he was assigned to inform on the three of us and report our conversations. When he was taken upstairs, he was fed instead of beaten. I don't know how Major became an informer. His father had been arrested when the Communists appropriated the oil wells that had been operated by the Standard Oil Company in western Hungary. His mother was a party secretary somewhere, and we knew that their home was full of pictures of Stalin and Rákosi. This should have given us a clue.

About a year later, the secret police officers who arrested and beat us were themselves arrested for embezzling. They had used forced laborers to build a luxury villa for their boss on Buda's most exclusive hill. I heard they were also accused of inventing criminal cases and conspiracies and arresting innocent people as a way of demonstrating their diligence and skill. Ours was one such made-up case. The secret policemen who handled our case were convicted, but we were not released.

· · ·

AFTER TWO WEEKS, we were handcuffed and transferred to the second floor of a semicircular building at the gates of a military school on the road leading from Budapest to Lake Balaton. (Today, whenever I go by car from Budapest to Balatonszemes, I pass in front of these cells.) We were each placed in a separate cell on the second floor. Only six of the original nine from Diósgyőr remained: György Schey had not been seen by anyone in the group since my draftsman days, and Tamás Major did not make the trip from the house near Váci Road. We did not know where Tamás Szemere was. A few days later, we learned how to communicate with one another through the walls. Here, too, we had to sleep on the floor without blankets. For the daily interrogations, we were led, one at a time, through a beautiful park to the second floor of a distant building. An enormous portrait of Lavrenty Beria, the head of the Soviet secret police and Stalin's heir, decorated the large entry hall.

My interrogator was a secret police officer I had not met before. Rather than beat me, he asked me if I knew where I was. He placed his officer's cap, with its distinctive blue secret police band, prominently on his desk so I would have no doubt about the location. When I told him that I had no idea why I was being held, he answered that my crime was so serious that if I did not confess, I would be hanged. Although he did not say so, I understood that the authorities' intent was to build a case that showed that people with relatives in the West were agents of the capitalist imperialists. Only later did I learn that six of us were accused of conspiring to blow up the Diósgyőr steel mill complex. Show trials based on such trumped-up charges were common in Stalin's day, as they served to illustrate that reactionary forces were constantly conspiring against the people and peace.

My interrogator told me he had the means to force my confession. To emphasize this threat, he turned his back to me, walked to a nearby window, and put his hands into his pants pockets, which lifted the back of his jacket to expose an enormous revolver stuck into his belt. But he was immediately frustrated because his jacket quickly fell back, covering the firearm. His efforts and his cheap theatrical trick were so ridiculous that I started laughing. When he turned around to face me, I expected a severe beating. Instead, he sent me back to my cell.

I soon realized that my situation was not only very serious but also perhaps hopeless. Later, while still in prison, I learned that my execution had already been announced. That's also when I first heard the specifics of the charge against me: I was a British spy who planned to blow up the Diósgyőr blast furnace, and I had become a spy because my parents lived in "Cleveland, Great Britain [sic]." Years later, I would meet old friends who were surprised to see me alive.

Some of Stalin's show trials served to eliminate real or potential rivals. Others were meant to demonstrate the necessity of subsequent purges or a new policy. At first, I suspected that our trial was supposed to prove that "the reactionary forces of the capitalist imperialist bloc planned to attack the Soviet Bloc. Therefore, those with relatives living in the West needed to be liquidated."

Meanwhile, unknown to us, momentous changes were taking place in Moscow. After Stalin's death, cracks appeared in the previously monolithic Soviet empire. First, workers in East Germany revolted. Russian troops quickly and cruelly put down this uprising. I learned about the East German rebellion during a chance encounter with forced laborers in the bathroom outside of my solitary cell.

Soon after the East German unrest, the Kremlin leaders started fighting with one another. Initially, the much-feared Lavrenty Beria consolidated all power in his hands and continued to rule with terror. The infighting culminated on June 25, 1953, when Nikita Khrushchev, allied with Minister of Defense Bulganin, Prime Minister Malenkov, Marshal Zhukov and his generals, and a few others, arrested Beria and took power. Beria and members of his circle were soon executed. General Batitsky personally put a bullet into the head of the screaming Beria. For this, Batitsky was later promoted to marshal. The new leaders blamed Beria for Stalin's excesses and instituted sweeping changes. They curbed the power of the secret police and released thousands of political prisoners. Stalin's favorites were replaced and sometimes eliminated. The new order improved all aspects of life in every corner of the Soviet empire.

In Hungary, the dictator Mátyás Rákosi was replaced with the moderate Imre Nagy. Nagy immediately instituted broad reforms, including, as noted earlier, deported people were now allowed to move anywhere in the country except to Budapest and five larger cities. The legal system was dramatically overhauled. Anyone who was arrested could not be held beyond a certain reasonable time without indictment and trial. Everyone locked up in Recsk and other secret internment camps were to be released immediately or indicted, tried, and released unless convicted. A general amnesty freed anyone sentenced to less than two years. All other sentences were reduced by one-third or, if issued by a military court, by one-half. Censorship was eased. Newspapers were allowed some freedom. Most important, the power of the secret police was greatly reduced.

All this seemed too good to be true. And it was. Unfortunately, Rákosi was able to hold on to the very important position of first secretary of the Communist Party. With the help of the secret police, he immediately started sabotaging Nagy's new orders. Eventually, the Stalinist wing of the party regained power, and the widely despised Rákosi replaced the very popular Imre Nagy in 1955. But in June 1953, this was all still ahead of us.

A few days after hearing about the East German uprising, I overslept in the morning. When I woke up, I realized from the sunlight on my wall that it was quite late, and that I should already be standing facing the wall. The sound of moaning from the next cell filtered ominously through the wall. They must have roughed up my friend Doleschál quite badly, I thought. Suddenly the chief officer of our guards, a sergeant, stepped into my cell. I started to get up and, as required, stand at attention, but he motioned that I should remain on the floor. He leaned on the door and started speaking: "I don't understand this world at all. We should beat you traitors and criminals and torture you, as you deserve. However, we got an order this morning to treat you like gentlemen. [He actually used the English word *gentlemen*.] Now what would you like for breakfast? How much coffee can you drink? How much bread can you eat? How much jam would you like with it? But don't ask for more than you can eat without getting sick. Listen to your friend next door. He just ate a whole loaf of bread."

I could not believe my ears. I told him that half a loaf would suffice. I also asked for jam. This was the first decent meal since my arrest more than a month earlier. The real surprise was lunch. The sergeant, still shaking his head in disbelief, brought us fried chicken with vegetables and, at the end, a delicious dessert. We were apparently being served what students at the military school ate. And from that day on, I no longer had to stand by the wall during daytime hours.

The interrogations ceased for a few days. When the grilling resumed, I noticed that the huge Beria portrait had disappeared from the lobby. The significance of this change was obvious. The interrogator was the same, but his behavior was now much less threatening. He asked me what I thought was the reason for my being there. I answered, "by mistake." He then asked me the reasons people were brought here. I searched my mind for a crime, any crime the secret police could not accuse me of. The only one I could think of was bigamy. He dismissed my answer and started listing the most heinous crimes, increasing the volume of his voice for each one. "For murder, for assassination, for spying, for conspiracy, for being a Trotskyite, for sabotage, for desertion, for robbery, for embezzlement, for rape, for beating up a policeman, for neglecting guard duty [forced laborers were part of the army], for subversive or antiparty activities." Here, he stood up, pointed his finger at me, and shouted at the top of his voice, "and for incitement against the state! And that is what you are here for!"

I knew that the maximum penalty for incitement against the state was only ten years, so I unconsciously sighed with relief. That surprised him. He then told me that the secret police knew everything about me and gestured toward a two-inch-thick manila folder on his desk.[13] He started paging through it randomly, stopping and reading every once in a while. "On such and such a date and hour, the accused, Sigmund Csicsery, said to other forced laborers that the party's newspaper, *Szabad Nép,* is only good for toilet paper." It was true. I did say that. "On another day, the accused joked that we are lucky that steamships have already been invented; otherwise we would be galley slaves." I had also said that.

From these details, I concluded that the informer must have been Tamás Major. Nevertheless, I admitted nothing. This game continued for several days. As I continued to maintain my innocence, I realized that the days of torture-extracted confessions and show trials were now over. Finally he told me, "Don't worry, we are not accusing you of plans to blow up a steel mill, and you can forget about hanging from the gallows. But keep in mind that the secret police never makes mistakes. You'll never get out of here without being convicted of something."

During the days that followed, we negotiated my situation. He read one statement after another that the informer had attributed to me. I denied all except those I considered the least offensive: the toilet paper statement, the galley-slave joke, and a few others. The most serious statement was that when I had learned of Stalin's death, I said, "It was no great loss" (*Nem kár érte*). That had also happened. I knew I had to admit to saying this last one after I was handcuffed and driven to another secret police prison, where I was confronted with my friend György Schey. I was deeply shocked. I had never seen anyone so badly beaten and broken. During an unguarded moment Schey whispered to me, "There is nothing more we can do. Admit what I say here." And when the interrogator asked him, my friend quoted my "no loss" statement. The interrogator then prepared my confession. I had to sign it.

The Fő Utca Military Prison

WITHIN DAYS, THE six of us were transferred to a huge prison, still in the city, on the corner of Fő and Gyorskocsi Streets. Major was free, Schey was somewhere in a prison, and we did not know where the ninth was. The secret police occupied half of this enormous building, and the other half was a military prison. On the army's side, the ground and first floors housed the offices of military prosecutors and judges, as well as other offices, storerooms, and the kitchen. The second floor housed a small hospital and additional medical facilities. The prison cells were on the upper floors. The gravity of the crime determined the floor to which a prisoner was assigned. Higher floors held inmates accused of more serious crimes. Murder, rape, falling asleep or having sex while on guard duty, disobeying orders, burglary, stealing, embezzlement, and other common crimes were the least serious crimes in a Communist society. Perpetrators of these crimes were on the third and fourth floors. Inmates on the higher floors were given less food and received harsher treatment than prisoners on the lower floors.

At first I was housed in a solitary cell, where I was allowed to sit on my plank bed. I spent most of my time praying, daydreaming, and meditating. I carved a chessboard on the plank bed and made little chess figures out of bread. I tried to play chess with myself but was unsuccessful, so I ate the chess figures. Every night armies of cockroaches invaded my cell. I wondered what they were looking for, as there was nothing for them to eat. I spent two weeks in solitary confinement in that cell.

One day I was led before a stern military judge. He read the confession I had signed and asked whether I had been forced to sign it. I should have said yes, but I feared that if I did, I would be handed back to the secret police. The sight of my friend György Schey still haunted me. I did not want to be treated like that. I told the judge that I had always been treated fairly. He looked disappointed and that surprised me. But it was too late, and I was led back to my cell. A few days after my appearance before the judge, I was thrown into a cell on the fifth floor, number 536, if I remember correctly. This cell already held about forty other prisoners.

All six of us were now on the fifth floor, the one reserved for political prisoners. Following Stalin's death, the secret police arrested thousands of people. Some were denounced and arrested for nothing more than a smile. The prisons were overflowing. The cells on the fifth floor were originally designed to hold about twelve convicts. Now, each one held at least three times that many. We slept in three-level bunk beds, with nine people occupying two such beds. Newcomers and younger inmates had to sleep in the middle, atop the dividing rods between two adjacent beds. I was a newcomer and much younger than most of the other prisoners, so I had to sleep in the middle. It was awful but still better than sleeping on a concrete floor. And now I had my own blanket.

Each cell had a hierarchy. A person's position on the totem pole was determined by a combination of time spent behind bars and the length of sentence, rather than military rank. Prisoners who had been arrested a long time ago looked down on us newcomers, saying that everyone arrested after them were not real Hungarians. In other words, we must have cooperated with the Communists to stay out of jail for so long.

The cell was my first encounter with other prisoners. The neighbor to my right was a well-educated young soldier. He knew a lot about both the prison system and what happens at trials and instructed me on how to behave. He told me about the other prisoners in our cell: whom to trust, whom to fear. He had spent some time in the secret police section of the building and related horror stories about what happened there: The prisoners were housed six or more in solitary cells and were forbidden to speak. Sleeping was difficult because powerful lamps illuminated each cell at night. Interrogations were usually held in the middle of the night and almost always involved torture. I learned from him, and also from other prisoners, that several people were executed almost every morning before Imre Nagy's reforms had been put into effect. New gallows were assembled during the evening in the prison's courtyard, the executions proceeded at daybreak, and then the gallows were disassembled. Imre Nagy halted the executions and ordered a review and retrial of all death penalty cases.

My neighbor to the left was Colonel Imre Surányi, a very nice army engineer. After the war, he was in charge of a plant that manufactured insulated electrical wire. When the Iron Curtain was constructed, the secret police purchased wire from the plant he supervised for the mines they laid along the border. He told them that the wire was good for indoor use only. Disregarding his warning, they installed the mines using his wire. When the wire corroded, someone had to be punished. Although he retained all the letters containing his warnings, he was convicted of sabotage and sentenced to a long prison term. When Imre Nagy reformed the justice system, Colonel Surányi's relatives hired a lawyer. His case was scheduled for retrial. He was sure he would be released.

Meals on the fifth floor at Fő Utca were not nearly as plentiful or nutritious as those in the military school's solitary cells had been. In the morning, we each received a half liter (about two cups) of coffee substitute. Rumor had it that bromide was put in our coffee to keep us pliant and obedient. We also got a daily bread ration of one loaf for every five prisoners. The bread was distributed following a strict ritual: One man cut the loaf into five equal slices, then each of the others took one piece. The last remaining fifth was the slicer's portion. The role of slicer and the picking order rotated daily. This system guaranteed that the division was fair. Some ate their entire portion at once; others kept small pieces for lunch and dinner. A diluted soup, most often cauliflower or kohlrabi and only occasionally potato, was lunch. Every once in a while, usually on holidays, we found a piece or two of chewy meat floating in it. Dinner was similar. We were always hungry.

This fare was bountiful compared to what was served on the sixth floor, however, where the so-called unfaithful ones (traitors) were kept. These unfortunates had no names, only numbers. They wore distinctive uniforms made from rough beige cloth. They also had to wear a hood-like cap that covered their faces so that nobody would recognize them. The guards treated the sixth-floor prisoners even more brutally than they treated us. Few survived there longer than six months, with most succumbing to tuberculosis.

According to the old-timers, in previous years, relatives could send food packages to prisoners. But when a high-ranking prison officer noticed sausages and bacon hanging in the cells, he promptly forbade the packages. Fortunately, it was a decision he lived to regret. He was arrested and was soon starving in one of the many prisons he had once supervised. Most probably he ended up on the losing side of one of the many power struggles within the Communist elite.

Every cell had a cell commander who maintained order and supervised the distribution of meals. The commander was either the highest-ranking military officer or the prisoner with the longest sentence. Ours was an air force master sergeant. He had served in the old army and knew my godfather, Gyula bácsi. After the war, he continued to serve in the new army. Apparently he was a good soldier, so the decision was made to promote him to officer, pending an investigation. Secret policemen went to his neighbors and asked about him. One neighbor, a Jewish woman, said that the master sergeant was a Nazi, and that at the end of 1944, he had killed both of her sons. Although he could prove that he was nowhere near Budapest in 1944 and that the woman never had any sons, he was sentenced to death. The Imre Nagy reforms gave him some hope, and his wife hired a lawyer who appealed his case. Nevertheless, he continued to live in the shadow of the gallows. All day he paced nervously back and forth in our little cell. I learned some time later that he was eventually acquitted. However, he was simultaneously convicted of incitement against the state. His new crime was a derogatory statement he made about the Communist justice system immediately after the judge read his death sentence at the first trial. For this second crime, he was sentenced to time served, so he was released from prison. But because of this second sentence, he could not receive any compensation for the years spent on death row.

Solárszky, a former classmate at the Technical University of Budapest, was accused of leading a group of three conspirators who planned to overthrow the regime. He was sentenced to death, only to be saved by Nagy's reforms. Solárszky was in another prison. The second member of his group, who was not much older than twenty, was in our cell. The secret police had tortured him so badly that all his hair had turned white. Later I met the third conspirator, a tram conductor. He was the one who informed me that my execution had been announced.

Krisztinkovics Pali bácsi was the most interesting character in our cell. He was an old gentleman who talked for hours about his travels around the world. After World War I, he had served in the Red Cross, where his assignment was to find and repatriate Hungarian POWs from Siberian camps. In those years, he also traveled to Mongolia and China. During World War II, he was part of a group of eleven code breakers. After the war, the Communist army asked the group to write a manual for future code breakers. When the manual that revealed all the secrets of their trade was completed, a new group took over their work. The secret police arrested all eleven members of the first group because they knew too much. They were treated brutally. After Imre Nagy's reforms, they were transferred from the torture chambers of the secret police to the military prison at Fő Utca, which was a big improvement. Each of them was placed in a separate cell to prevent communication among them. Because the group had eleven members, we called them "the soccer team." I learned from Pali bácsi that one of the eleven, Béla Ujfalussy (1897–1987), was a relative of mine. His wife, Róza Erdőteleki Kovács (1906–83), was my mother's cousin.

Occasionally the prisoners from the fifth floor were taken to the prison courtyard for fresh air and exercise. For about half an hour, we marched around in absolute silence, as mingling with prisoners from other cells was strictly forbidden. Nevertheless, a few times I managed to fall behind our group and talk with Béla bácsi.

As noted earlier, Imre Nagy's reforms of that summer included freeing those imprisoned without trial or conviction, among them the inmates of the Recsk internment camp. But only a few of them were released. Most of the others remained incarcerated, accused of some new crime. They were tried, found guilty, and received long prison sentences. Each cell on the fifth floor housed a few of these unfortunates. I heard a famous escape story from one of them.

The Recsk internees worked in a quarry six days a week. Housekeeping and similar chores were done on Sundays. Each Sunday, guards with submachine guns escorted groups of about a dozen inmates into the nearby forest to gather firewood. One group secretly fabricated an authentic-looking secret police uniform and then carved a fake submachine gun out of wood and painted it black with shoe polish. The next Sunday morning, the group marched through the gate with the other groups and then melted away into the forest. The guards did not discover that one of the firewood-gathering groups had not returned until the afternoon. Unfortunately, all but one escapee were recaptured. The man who got away was able to cross the border into Austria. He had memorized the names of all the inmates at Recsk, and the list of names was read over Radio Free Europe. The saddest part of the story is that people in the West did not believe what he revealed about the horrors of the Recsk camp. They could not accept that the Communists maintained such cruel camps in total secrecy. His escape did have at least one positive result: some of the relatives of the secretly disappeared prisoners now knew their loved ones were still alive.

Some forty or fifty of the Recsk inmates were former railroad employees. Western radio stations such as the BBC and Voice of America periodically broadcasted how many cattle, how much wheat and other produce, and how many industrial products moved from Hungary to Russia at the Csap border station. (Csap is now Chop and is part of Ukraine.) Because the publicized numbers were accurate, the secret police arrested people who had access to the figures, the railroad men. Despite the fact that the news continued after the arrests, proving that none of those arrested had been leaking the data, the railroad men were sent to Recsk rather than released. To have done otherwise would have suggested the secret police could be wrong. When the Nagy reforms closed the Recsk camp, these same prisoners, rather than being released, were sentenced to many more years on various trumped-up charges. I heard this story from several of the former railroad people but have no other verification of its accuracy.

The fifth floor also held men who had fought in Southeast Asia. In 1945, many young Hungarians, fleeing the advancing Soviet army, went to Austria and Germany. When they could not find jobs, they enlisted in the French Foreign Legion, and some of them subsequently served in the First Indochina War. After the French surrender at Dien Bien Phu, the Vietnamese army repatriated most of the captured Hungarian legionnaires to Hungary. The Hungarian government meted out long prison sentences to these "imperialist mercenaries" because they had fought with the capitalist French forces against the peaceful, freedom-loving Vietnamese people.

Some of these ex-legionnaires sported tattoos. On the chest of one of them was the image of an Arab holding the reins of a camel under a palm tree. This turned out to be a popular choice. In almost every cell, four or five others tattooed the same drawing on their chest or upper arm. These copycats used medicinal charcoal for the dye. I have no idea where they got needles. Other common tattoo subjects were girlfriends' names and curvaceous nudes.

After the war, the Russians took a very large number of Hungarian civilians for "a little labor" (*malenkij robot*). Some were released at the end of the day, though others were taken to Siberian labor camps in the Gulag. After four or five years, those who survived the ordeal were released. As they returned, the Hungarian secret police promptly arrested most of them at the border because "the Russians would not have taken them had they not been war criminals or dangerous enemies of Communism." Soldiers returning from prisoner-of-war camps were similarly convicted of some crime and spent many more years in prison. Several of these former POWs were in our cell. Colonel Kondor was one of them. I had met his daughter, Kati, at Kőbányai Gyógyszer-gyár during the summer of 1950. She was a technician and assisted me in one of my projects. Kati told me that her father disappeared during the war in Russia, and the family had not heard from him since. Colonel Kondor was very happy when I told him that his daughter was alive and well and living in Budapest.

A few months later, I was being transported with a handful of other prisoners on a public bus. Although we were handcuffed to one another, we were seated with the other passengers. I was pleasantly surprised when I saw Tibor Wein, a chemical engineer at Kőbányai Gyógyszergyár and a good friend of mine, boarding our section of the bus. Fortunately he noticed me and managed to take the seat next to me. The guards were half asleep, so we could talk to each other. I told him why I was a prisoner and how we were treated. I told him that I had met Colonel Kondor, as well, and he promised to tell Kati that her father was alive and in good health at the Fő Utca prison.

One of the most interesting stories I heard at the time was about a people-smuggling operation run by the miller in the Hungarian village of Rajka, which lies next to the Austrian border. Would-be escapees had to deposit half of the required money in a Swiss bank and pay the other half directly to the miller and his assistant in Hungary. The two smugglers floated down the Danube at night from Austria to Hungary, using just a small boat. They collected their clients in Budapest and somehow smuggled them into Austria. The prisoner did not tell me how they succeeded in crossing into Austria with such large groups, but they made several successful round trips. Their last attempt involved about forty people.

As that final operation started, they had already contacted all but two of the forty. The last two, an elderly couple, lived inside the Dutch embassy. Before the war, the husband had been undersecretary of transportation. The miller and his helper debated about whether to telephone them for two reasons: they suspected the embassy phones were bugged, and the wife, who was unable to walk long distances, had requested a sled, which would make crossing the border even more difficult. They finally made the call and then went to see a film at a nearby theater. The secret police arrested them as they left the theater and found the list of the addresses of all forty would-be escapees on them. Everyone on the list was rounded up and given long prison sentences. The miller of Rajka was hanged, but because the assistant was from Czechoslovakia and was not a Hungarian citizen, he could not be executed. He was instead imprisoned for life.

The tale of a fellow prisoner, a young peasant army recruit, was one of the saddest stories I heard. The boy's mother had lost her eyesight when she gave birth to him. A successful operation some two decades later restored her sight, and the mother now wished to see her son, who was serving in the army at the time. She wrote him, asking him to request a leave and come home for a few days. When his commanding officer refused the request, the boy went home anyway. He was sentenced to many years in prison.

Every prison cell also held several Gypsies and a few common criminals, such as thieves, embezzlers, robbers, and murderers. They liked to entertain us with colorful stories of their exploits. These tales invariably emphasized the high level of skill they demonstrated in their criminal calling, always insisting they were caught only because of some extraordinary combination of circumstances or because some bastard betrayed them. If these accounts were true, our cell housed the best burglar, the best thief, the best pickpocket, and so on. This group adhered to a rigid caste system, too, with safecrackers and bank robbers the aristocracy, robbers the middle class, and rapists the outcasts.

These inmates also spoke a prison slang, much of which was derived from Yiddish or Romany words. Among the most popular words in their lexicon were *piálni* (to drink) and *kajálni* (to eat), which came from the Romany language,[14] and *smasszer* (warden, prison guard), which was taken from Yiddish.[15] The words *vamzer* (snitch, informer) and *hipis* (searching the prisoners and their cell) may have had Yiddish origins, as well. There were also more or less standardized expressions that stood for simple words. For example, "Tudod mit mondott a missziós pap? Hát a faszom nem kéne?" (Do you know what the missionary said? Why don't you just suck my cock!) was a strong refusal of a request or response to a question. Young prisoners who wanted to look cool or sophisticated were quick to use this slang. But because more and more people of all ages were spending time in prison, its use was soon picked up by others, so that even older political prisoners adopted it. Eventually, this distinctive vocabulary spread outside the prisons and entered the Hungarian language.

The Gypsies contributed more than colorful stories to the prison environment. They were a noisy group who would sing and dance for hours, which some of the other prisoners liked because it distracted them from their miserable fate. They frequently squabbled among themselves, too. Although they would occasionally steal one another's bread, I never heard of them stealing anything from non-Gypsy prisoners. Several were illiterate, and most of them were in prison because of some petty crime or act of insubordination.

One of the Gypsies, whose bed was not far from mine, had an interesting story. One afternoon he was on guard duty. On the way home from a nearby plant, some workers teased him: "Gypsy, are you proud that you are now a guard in the People's

Army?" He threw his helmet and rifle down, cursed his guard duty, cursed the army, and in no uncertain terms asked the workers to tell Mihály Farkas, the minister of defense, to have sex with his mother. An informer in the crowd reported this to his superior, and he was promptly arrested.

Bedbugs added to everyone's misery regardless of status, and there was not much anyone could do about them. We did discover, however, that the higher the floor, the fewer the bedbugs. According to one of several theories, prisoners on the upper floors got less food, which meant they had less blood for the bugs to suck. Another explanation was that political prisoners washed themselves more often than common criminals.

Some of the guards, like the bedbugs, added to everyone's misery. The ones who stood in the hallways and escorted us during weekly exercise walks in the courtyard were conscripted privates. They held submachine guns ready to fire but never spoke a word. They were probably forbidden to talk to us. Most of the professional wardens were old and were already wardens before the Communist takeover. They treated us the same as they treated the thieves, robbers, and murderers of the prewar years, and during my time in the prison, they never beat any of us. We were also overseen by many sergeants from the military, most of whom had been transferred to the prison from the army. Unlike the professional wardens, they were aware that we were political prisoners, which made some of them very uncomfortable. They were friendly and tried to ease our suffering as much as possible. Later, when I worked at the prison hospital, I got to know several of these good guards well. They often came to our rooms to rest and chitchat during breaks, and they talked to us openly.

A number of the sadistic guards also came from the army, while others were midrank secret police. They regularly harassed us with nocturnal searches, or *hipis*. We had to line up and place all of our clothes and meager belongings on the floor in front of us. Permitted items were a toothbrush and toothpaste, a spoon and fork, and a mess kit and a cup. We had to empty the straw sacks on which we slept. Then the order came that an inspection would occur at such and such a time. We had to refill the straw sacks very fast and, after they were restuffed, clean the floor.

After the new Soviet leadership restored relations with Tito in Yugoslavia, the Serbian political prisoners were released. A week later, a group of these former Serbian prisoners caught one of our most sadistic guards on the street and beat him up so badly that he had to be treated in a mental hospital. Another guard—we called him "the parachutist" because he wore small parachutes on his lapel— was chased through the streets. By the time he reached the prison gates, he had lost both of his shoes. A few days later, one of our "good" guards told us that he was standing in a crowd somewhere when someone recognized him and loudly announced the presence of a *smasszer* (prison guard). "Let's beat him up!" the crowd roared. What surprised the guard most was that three people in this small crowd immediately protested the call, saying that they knew him, that he was a good guy, and that he should be treated with respect. In those days, even a small crowd included at least half a dozen former political prisoners, a fact that was reflected in a popular saying of the time: there are three types of people in Hungary, those who have been in prison, those who are there now, and those who will be there soon.

But it was not only the guards who limited our access to the world. Slanted sheet-metal plates that permitted light and air to enter the cells but blocked our view of the outdoors covered every upper-floor window. Some years earlier, a high-ranking Communist had noticed convicts standing by each prison window looking out into the streets. He did not like what he saw because he knew it made sign language communication possible between convicts and their families or other free citizens. He also knew that free people who had been indoctrinated to believe that only a small number of their compatriots were behind bars should not see how crowded the prisons really were. An order was promptly issued to install sheet-metal plates over the windows in every prison. While he was a prisoner at Vác, the poet Tibor Tollas wrote a beautiful poem, *Bebádogoznak minden ablakot . . .* (They're boarding up all the windows . . .), that describes the result. His poem ends with a warning to the free world.

S Váctól Pekinging zúgják a rabok:
Ha nem vigyáztok, az egész világon
Bebádogoznak minden ablakot!

[From Vác to Peking, prisoners cry out;
if you don't watch out, they will board up
all the windows in the world!]

• • •

ONE DAY, I was led to a jovial master sergeant in the prison hospital. He explained that the prisoner pharmacist had left and a new one was needed. He had checked my files and had seen that I had once worked at a pharmaceutical plant. Would I object to taking over the pharmacist's duties? he asked. I gladly volunteered. Then he whispered that his superiors did not like letting a political prisoner work in such an important post. They would have preferred and trusted a thief or a murderer, but he had fought to choose me. "Be careful," he whispered. "Every word you say and everything you do will be watched." I was to discuss any problems I encountered only with him. He told me whom to trust and whom to fear in the hospital. As we became more acquainted with each other, I saw what an extraordinarily good person he was.

CHAPTER NINE

The Prison Hospital (1953)

I MOVED TO the prison hospital to assume my new job as prisoner pharmacist. One large room served as the office for the doctors and the dentist. My desk and the medicine cabinets were also there. Sick prisoners were confined in a row of small cells next to the clinic. The so-called unfaithful (traitors) from the sixth floor were kept in separate cells, and I was instructed not to speak to them when I gave them medicine. Each time I entered one of their cells, a guard with a submachine gun stood next to me to ensure that I didn't say a single word. Another cell housed one or two sick female prisoners.

The hospital was run by a Dr. Meyer, who wore the uniform of a regular army officer. He was probably a competent doctor but was very cruel. Among themselves, prisoners called him Dr. Mengele, after the infamous Nazi doctor known for his medical experiments on living people in the concentration camps.

The prisoner doctor was a nice young man from Mohács, a town a few hours south of Budapest. The army had drafted him as a doctor, and his chief nurse was an informer and had denounced him. I recall that his sentence was four or five years. We soon became good friends.

Another prisoner on the medical staff was a young medic from Kál, a small village north of Lake Balaton. He became my other friend at the infirmary. One day I told him a story about the summer of 1947, when my cousin Zoltán, another friend, and I had bicycled around Lake Balaton. We stopped to rest by a little lake, and because it was a hot afternoon, we took a dip. As soon as we got in the water, dozens of large black leeches attacked us, so we made a hasty retreat. He was not at all surprised and explained that the lake was famous for these large leeches. At the time, doctors used leeches to suck blood from people who had high blood pressure. The leeches also injected hirudin, a chemical that both slows coagulation and lowers blood pressure. Older people around Kál earned money catching and selling the leeches. They would put their legs in the water until they were covered with leeches, and then remove the leeches from their skin with salty water.

For our bedroom, the prisoner doctor, the medic from Kál, and I used a large room next to the clinic, which we shared with one or two sick prisoners. An elderly prisoner, also a doctor, was a permanent resident. We were told he was ailing, and although he spent all of his time in bed, he appeared to be quite healthy. My benefactor, the good master sergeant, had once been his coachman, and he somehow managed to keep his old boss safely in the hospital. We liked him. He told interesting stories and had a good sense of humor. After the war, he had shared an apartment with the very famous and beautiful actress and singer Katalin Karády. When one of us commented that this must have been wonderful, he said that it wasn't because she secretly ate his fruit preserves.

Life was good. We slept in real beds on real mattresses with white sheets. There was enough to eat. Even the wardens treated us with some respect.

The wardens brought sick prisoners to the clinic every morning, and Dr. Meyer or the prisoner physician examined them. I took notes and then recorded the diagnosis and treatment. Later, I dispensed the medication. In the afternoons and evenings, I had time to read. The only books available were about medicine. The first book I started reading was about internal medicine, and I immediately made a horrible discovery: I had the typical symptoms of several incurable and debilitating diseases that after inflicting long and painful suffering were always fatal. Descriptions of these maladies started with the same statement: "During the first months or years, patients have no symptoms and the malady is undetectable." I didn't get much sympathy from my doctor friend when I asked him what, if anything, I could do. He said I was a hypochondriac and should find something else to read.

One day I recognized one of the women prisoners waiting for treatment. She was Sardagna Ata néni. Her son, Hansi, had been a high school classmate and good friend of mine in Kassa. Dr. Meyer was present, so I never succeeded in speaking with her. Twenty years later, we met at her son's home in Basel, Switzerland.

Another elderly woman was so sick that she needed hospitalization. They put her into one of the solitary cells next to the clinic. I found out that she was one of the forty would-be escapee clients of the miller from Rajka. It was she and her husband who had been living in the Dutch embassy and to whom the miller had made his fateful telephone call. She constantly pestered us, requesting that her girlfriend—also a convict at Fő Utca—share her cell because she was bored and lonely. She refused to understand that we, too, were prisoners.

At noontime one day, the cook who distributed our lunches called me by name. I was surprised and asked him how he knew who I was. He was the younger brother of Dénes Dicházi, another high school classmate of mine in Kassa. Both Dénes and his brother had become secret police officers. The brother's men had roughed up some visiting East German workers, and he took the fall after East German authorities complained. Now he was a convict.

One afternoon, a group of high-ranking officers brought a handcuffed young man into the clinic. I was there alone sorting some pills. An obviously angry officer demanded that I check the prisoner's breath for alcohol. I produced a manual and explained the procedure: I would prepare a dilute solution of potassium permanganate and ask the man to blow into the solution. Alcohol in the man's breath would cause the purple color to fade. If his breath did not change the deep purple of the permanganate solution, the man was sober. I weighed out the potassium permanganate and water in front of the officers and then prepared the solution. I asked the officers to wait for a few minutes. They withdrew and talked to one another. The young man stood next to me and, in a very low voice, told me his story. He was the best fighter pilot in the air force. One day he and a few others had to compete with visiting Russian pilots. Instead of using real bullets, they filmed how many shots would have hit the enemy. At the competition, he scored better than the best Russian fighter pilot. His mistake was in not knowing that he was supposed to lose. He was arrested and sentenced to several years in prison.

When Imre Nagy reformed the legal system, the army's judiciary reexamined and retried his case at a provincial city in eastern Hungary. He was acquitted and immediately released. Many of his former officer friends were present at the trial, and after his release, they drank some wine at a lunch celebrating his acquittal. After lunch, they let him fly a two-seater to Budapest. He offered to take the prosecutor, the same man who a few hours earlier had made every effort to keep him incarcerated, with him for the flight, and the prosecutor accepted his generous offer. On the way to Budapest, the pilot flew loops and corkscrews, which caused the prosecutor to throw up and to feel as if he might die. Immediately after landing, the prosecutor had the pilot arrested and charged with flying under the influence of alcohol. I quietly assured him that he should not worry because the solution would not fade no matter how much he had imbibed. I did not tell him that while preparing the test solution, I used ten times more potassium permanganate than required. I asked the officers to observe the test. The young pilot blew into the solution, and the color did not change. We repeated the test a few times. The results were always negative. His handcuffs were removed and he walked out a free and happy man. We never saw each other again.

Part of the army's judiciary branch occupied the ground floor of our building, and the same dentist who periodically visited us also treated these people. When the dentist came, I was always assigned to assist him. One frequent dental patient was the judge who would later preside at my trial, and on the occasions when he was being treated, we would talk with each other. He seemed to be a decent man.

At the end of summer, Dr. Meyer took a two-week vacation. His substitute, an army doctor from a nearby garrison, arrived with a big smile. He sent everyone else out of the clinic and seated the prisoner doctor, the medic, and me next to him. He emptied his bulging pockets and presented us with sausages, candy bars, and other delicacies. Then he sent us to the fifth floor where the political prisoners were housed and told us to put as many prisoners on double rations as possible. He was not allowed to do anything with those on the sixth floor. He warned us that these double rations would last only for the two weeks Dr. Meyer was away.

While studying the lists of prisoners, I found that my friend György Schey was now in one of the cells. During those two weeks, in addition to writing his name on the double-rations list, I put him on the sick list several times. Whenever the guards brought him to the clinic, I managed to separate him from the others by weighing him, taking his blood pressure, or performing some other unnecessary test. I gave him some of my sausages and several kinds of vitamins. His tears flowed while he swallowed large spoonfuls of foul-tasting cod liver oil. But he knew that after months without sunshine he needed it, and he thanked me. We were also able to talk unobserved. He told me that at my trial he would withdraw his testimony. I asked him not to, as it would not help me but would certainly harm him. He said he had made up his mind that he would not cooperate with these cruel gangsters.

A few days after Dr. Meyer returned from vacation, he ordered me to accompany him to the sixth floor. He would be examining the sick, and I was to record what he dictated. He warned me that while I was there I should keep my eyes on my notepad. I should never, no matter what happened, raise my eyes and look at any of the traitors. When we arrived on the sixth floor, we went into a very small room near the stairway. Armed guards led the sick prisoners, one at a time, into the room.

The prisoners had only numbers, no names. Some were so weak that two others had to carry them. I could see little more than their legs, most of them badly swollen from hunger edema. The little skin I saw was an unnatural gray. Some of the patients had advanced cases of tuberculosis. One man explained that he was once a secret police physician and that he now had Bechterev's disease (Ankylosing spondylitis) and that his vertebrae would soon fuse together unless he exercised. But starvation had so weakened him that he could not exercise. Would Dr. Meyer, his former colleague, put him on double rations for a few weeks? When he finished his plea, Dr. Meyer dictated to me, "Healthy. No treatment necessary." And this was his decision in every case. Not a single one of the clearly very sick men received any medication or treatment. I could not sleep that night, and years later I still had nightmares about the experience.

One day the guards brought a very sick woman to one of the solitary cells next to the clinic. She had a serious kidney infection and was about to die. She was obviously a traitor, as she had no name, just a number, and whenever we had to treat her or give her medication, we had to call a guard to be present before entering her cell. Despite the high level of secrecy, we learned that she was the wife of József Bekes. Two or three years earlier, a secret police unit had chased a Yugoslav spy into a village near the Yugoslav border. During the chase, the spy hid in one of the houses and then ran through the backyards of a dozen others before crossing the border. The secret police arrested all of the people who were in the house where the spy had rested and also the owners of the lots he had crossed. Mrs. Bekes owned one of the houses where the spy had stayed. She and several others were condemned to death. The others drew very long prison sentences.

Everyone who was sentenced to death was hung except for Mrs. Bekes, as she was pregnant at the time and could not be executed until after giving birth. When she gave birth, the state immediately took away the child, but her execution was further delayed because she contracted a severe kidney infection. Dr. Meyer gave her his personal attention, doing his best to save her life. This was not out of altruism. We learned that Dr. Meyer had made a bet with someone that he could cure this traitorous woman so she could be hung. We prayed every day that God would not allow Dr. Meyer to win his bet. Mrs. Bekes died peacefully in her sleep a few days later.

CHAPTER TEN

Trials (1953)

OUR DAY IN court finally arrived. The first trial was held in early August 1953 at the Budapesti Hadbiróság (Budapest Military Court), the charges were incitement against the state, and the case was listed as Sigmund Csicsery and Accomplices.[16] Apparently, my crimes were more serious than those committed by my five accomplices.

Sándor Ray, my court-appointed lawyer, had contacted my uncle Gábor bácsi and offered his services, saying he would conduct a better-than-average defense for me. Mr. Ray always wore the party emblem on his lapel and talked a lot, but he failed to inspire Gábor bácsi's confidence. There was too little time before the trial to retain a different attorney, however, so he accepted his services. János Tuschák's relatives had more time to pick and choose and hired the best of the few defense lawyers acceptable to the military court, a Mr. Glatz.

The judge was a decent man by the name of Mundi, and I had the impression that he wanted to acquit us. György Korda, who was twenty-four or twenty-five years old, was the prosecutor. A friend of mine who had attended law school with him told me that Korda was the most bloodthirsty Communist in their class.

Among Imre Nagy's reforms was the legalization of justice, one result of which was that every trial now required a jury. The military jury had two members, an officer and an enlisted man, and these two young men did not hide their sympathies. They talked to us during breaks and assured us they would vote in our favor.

Mr. Robert Zentel, technical director at the Forte photo-chemical factory at Vác, provided brilliant testimony about my devotion to my work, my wonderful accomplishments, and so on. This visibly impressed the judge and the two jurors.

I was also allowed to say a few words in my own defense. I, too, emphasized my dedication to my work and then added that I had never said anything harmful. When I finished, Korda mockingly asked the judge and the jurors, "Would you believe anything said by the son of an ex-army officer now living in the West?"

The secret police officer who interrogated and regularly beat us during the first two weeks of our confinement was sitting in the audience. When János Tuschák's lawyer, Mr. Glatz, noticed him, he objected to his presence, and the judge had the officer removed.

The prosecutor then called György Schey to testify against me. As he had promised, Schey told the judge that he was forced to make the deposition against me and not a single word of it was true. The prosecutor asked the judge to halt the trial. As Schey was led out of the court, he had to pass next to Korda, who whispered to him, "You just got yourself another four years!"

György Schey's case was separate from ours. I later learned that he spent two or three more years in prison than the rest of us. He escaped to Israel in 1956, completed medical school, and became a physician. In 1986, while attending a conference in Israel, I found out that he had become a lung specialist and was the director of a hospital in Tel Aviv. I was able to call and thank him for his sacrifice. Unfortunately, we were unable to meet during the short time I was there. Of all the people I ever met, I admire him most for his uncompromising bravery.

Our trial continued on August 18, 1953. Gábor bácsi and Dóra néni attended. The prosecutor produced a new witness to testify against me. It was Tamás Szemere (no relation to the family of Gabrielle Szemere, who would later become my wife), and he had been among the nine forced laborers transferred from Diósgyőr to Budapest. I noticed his arm was in a cast. He said, "Yes, I definitely remember Sigmund Csicsery said. . . ." He then listed the statements in the court charges, ending with, "and I even remember the exact date." He then gave a date weeks after my arrest!

At the end of the testimony, I had the right to say a few words on my own behalf. I asked the judge to check the date of our arrest. He did. I then said that Tamás Szemere's statements couldn't be true because I was already in custody on the date he provided.

My lawyer spoke for five or ten minutes. He summarized what Robert Zentel had said and repeated the inconsistency in Tamás Szemere's testimony. The court had appointed him to defend three of the other defendants, as well. He pled leniency for them because of their tender years. Mr. Glatz's defense most likely saved Tuschák and probably benefited all of us.

During lunch, the judge was away for far too long, perhaps two or three hours. When the trial resumed, he and the two jurors retired to decide the verdict. They returned five minutes later, and the judge proceeded to read the verdicts. This took over a half hour. First, he listed our crimes. Then he said that the lack of any evidence that I ever committed a crime was a mitigating circumstance. Therefore, he sentenced me to a mere two years and four months in prison, to be followed by the loss of my civil rights for two more years, during which I could not vote or be elected to public office. Imre Nagy's amnesty automatically cut my sentence in half. Since the prosecutor had asked for the most severe punishment allowed by law, and inciting was punishable by up to ten years in prison, my sentence was lighter than I had expected.

László Doleschál was also sentenced to two years and four months. János Tuschák, Miklós Miletics, and the other two defendants received only two years. Those sentenced to two years or less were immediately released under a provision of Imre Nagy's amnesty. Not surprisingly, the prosecutor appealed for harsher punishments and the lawyers appealed for more lenient ones. (I was not unhappy to learn that later, after Imre Nagy reformed the judicial system, György Korda was transferred to a minor post in the countryside as retribution for his excessive prosecutorial zeal.)

László Doleschál and I were led back to our cells. We theorized that during his extraordinarily long lunch break, the judge had gone to the secret police to negotiate the verdicts. We knew that he and the two jurors could not have composed a text in five minutes that required a half hour to read, which could only mean that despite "the age of legalization," sentences were still decided by the secret police. Yet our judge probably fought the secret police on our behalf. The sentences we were handed could have been the result of a compromise.

Our theory proved true. Sometime after I regained my freedom, I accidentally met Judge Mundi in Buda, and he told me that the appeals court should have released László Doleschál and me. That this did not happen was just bad luck.

Our case was appealed to the Katonai Felsöbiróság (Upper Military Court) and a hearing was scheduled for a few weeks later at a beautiful villa in an elegant section of Buda. Dóra néni attended. We were able to talk freely until the hearing began. Finally, a clerk announced that the judge could not attend and the trial was postponed to October 21.

On October 20, an announcement was made that several hundred of us prisoners had volunteered to work in coal mines. I immediately reported that I could not volunteer because my appeal was scheduled for the next day. The warden's reply was that all that would happen is that I would get a more severe punishment, and that I should go to the mines. I refused, so I was chained and dragged to a truck that took us away.

The hearing was held as scheduled the next day. Because neither Doleschál nor I was present and our lawyer had forgotten to attend, the appeals court did not change our sentences.[17] Comrade Ray forgot to attend my trial but he did not forget to bill me 1,000 forints, about double what my monthly salary had been as a chemical engineer at Forte.

CHAPTER ELEVEN

Markó Street Prison and the Coal Mine (1953)

INSTEAD OF GOING to a coal mine, the truck took us to the Markó Street prison in Pest. There were six of us in one cell: Dr. Móhr, the army's chief surgeon; a retired undersecretary of transportation; an accomplice of my former classmate, Solárszky; a Jehovah's Witness; an old farmer; and me.

A couple of years after this initial meeting, Dr. Móhr and I lived in the same apartment house. His wife was Györgyi Botond, Hungary's most famous figure skater. During the 1956 revolution, when my fiancée, Gabi, and I decided to escape from Hungary on foot, Gabi had no walking shoes, so Mrs. Móhr gave Gabi her boots.

The retired undersecretary was one of the would-be escapees arrested with the miller of Rajka (see chapter eight). He was the husband of the couple the miller had telephoned at the Dutch embassy the night before the group was scheduled to leave, a call that had resulted in everyone being arrested. I had already met the undersecretary's wife when she was a patient at the prison hospital (see chapter nine), and the old gentleman was happy to learn that his wife had recovered. Two years later, we ran into each other again in Budapest on Szent István Ring Road, and he told me that his wife had died.

Solárszky's accomplice had been a bus driver before he was arrested. After graduating from high school, he had wanted to continue his studies, but was refused admission to any university because of his middle-class background. We soon became good friends.

On our second or third day together, the retired undersecretary proposed that every day after lunch one of us give an hour-long lecture about something in his field. He talked about life during the Habsburg monarchy, as he liked the Habsburgs and disliked everything that followed the fall of the monarchy. Dr. Móhr talked about how to make large breasts smaller and small breasts larger and more beautiful. The Jehovah's Witness talked about his faith and tried his best to convert us. The old farmer, whose crime was that his son had successfully escaped through the Iron Curtain, thought our talks were unnecessary and did not participate. I talked about how photographic film worked and how it was manufactured. I don't remember my bus driver friend's subject, but he observed that the undersecretary invariably fell asleep five minutes after each lecture started. We concluded that he couldn't sleep until someone started to give a scientific lecture.

After a little more than a week, I and a few other prisoners were shipped to a coal mine.

The Szuhakálló, Szeles Akna Coal Mine

Szuhakálló is north of the large industrial city of Miskolc, in Borsod-Abaúj-Zemplén County, northeastern Hungary. Szeles Akna (Windy Mine) was a small mine that, in addition to a handful of civilian professional miners, employed slightly over three hundred prisoners. The mine's poor-quality brown coal had a very high ash content, and the coal layer was relatively thin. The rock above the coal seam was composed of ancient clam fossils. I never found out the age of the fossils. The entire compound was surrounded by a barbwire fence, and day and night, armed guards in tall towers along the fence watched us.

Soon after our small group arrived from Budapest, I was happy to see several friends from the Fő Utca prison, including my former cellmate Imre Surányi. Imre bácsi told me that the wardens had put him in charge of all the machinery and electrical equipment in the mine because he was an engineer. He put me in charge of a winch that hoisted a miner's trolley up a steep shaft from a Russian-made supermachine that was supposed to produce more coal than several dozen miners. On the rare occasions the machine worked, I was kept busy handling the winch and transferring the coal to the train that took it to the surface. However, this pride of Russian engineering broke down almost every day. Much of the time I had nothing to do but sit in the dark, daydreaming or sleeping.

A handful of professional miners worked with us. Their job was to teach us the difficult skills of mining. They always treated us as equals, not as prisoners. These men worked six days a week, while the prisoner-miners had to work seven days a week. There were three shifts: 6 a.m. to 2 p.m., 2 p.m. to 10 p.m., and 10 p.m. to 6 a.m., with a change over the weekend. This meant that every third week, one-third of us had sixteen-hour shifts. The shift change did not affect the professional miners because they did not work on Sundays. Longer shifts led to laxer attention spans that resulted in several accidents, some fatal. The most common accidents were being hit by a runaway miner's trolley and not being able to jump away fast enough from a large piece of falling coal or rock. But prisoners were expendable, and this schedule remained intact during my tenure at the mine.

We used acetylene-gas lamps (carbide lamps). Adjusting the amount of water dripping on the carbide sets its brightness. Most of us wore leather helmets, which were useful for working or walking in dark, tight spaces. East German–made helmets of hard plastic were also available. They offered better protection than the leather helmets and initially were more popular. However, when we noticed that something in the plastic was making our hair fall out, most of us switched back to the old leather helmets.

Most prisoner-miners worked either on the "front," striking at the coal wall with a pickax or shoveling coal onto a conveyor belt. Others worked with the professional miners in the construction of new shafts. This work consisted of drilling holes roughly two feet (60 cm) deep for dynamite, calling the professional who handled the explosives, withdrawing to a safe distance during the explosion, shoveling the broken-up coal into a trolley, and finally, building the wooden structure to hold up the ceiling over the newly created extension of the shaft.

We weren't alone in the mine. There were rats. The professional miners liked them because they believed the rats could sense dangerous gas levels. Some even brought food for them. Fortunately, our mine had no gas and therefore no danger of a gas explosion.

Various molds and fungi grew in the older shafts and on the wooden elements holding up the shafts. Several of these emitted a faint ghostly light, most visible when a lamp was accidentally extinguished.

The two rows of barracks that housed the prisoners were near the entrance to the mine. They were reasonably comfortable, with small iron stoves providing heat during the winter. We had as much coal as we could smuggle out of the mine, so the barracks were always overheated. I didn't like sleeping in that heat, but most of the others did. There was a library, and I spent most of my free time reading. In addition to political books, there were works like Stendhal's *The Red and the Black*.

Being a miner is a physically exhausting job, and miners need to consume about five thousand calories per day to be effective. The authorities recognized that they had to feed us well, so our rations were simple but nutritious and sufficient.

Several of the wardens were Tirpáks, members of a small Magyar-speaking group whose Slovak ancestors had settled in northeastern Hungary about three centuries ago. Most of them were poorly educated. The older professional wardens treated us as common criminals. One afternoon, one of the sergeants had to write my name into a notebook. He wrote down a C, then stopped. After a short time, he said, "My hand is very tired today. You finish the rest of your name."

I met an interesting cross-section of Hungarian society at the mine, ranging from the upper classes to the criminal underworld. The inmates included a few aristocrats; many professionals, tradesmen, shop owners and small business owners; and a surprisingly large number of factory workers, farmers, and landless peasants. Many ex-soldiers and former policemen were in the mix, as well. There were cliques among the prisoners, too. For example, officers of the old army who had fought against the Russians in World War II seldom mingled with the officers of the new Communist army.

The diversity of the population was no surprise. At one point I read that between 1950 and 1953, at the height of the terror, the courts produced 387,000 guilty verdicts. This was more than 5 percent of Hungary's adult population. And this number did not include the people imprisoned without trial or conviction. The Communist Party classified everyone who fought between 1941 and 1945 as a war criminal. As a result, little Hungary had more war criminals than Germany and Italy combined. Kangaroo courts condemned thousands of these unfortunates to long prison terms. Hundreds of others were executed. There were also some common criminals—thieves, robbers, murderers—at the mine.

In theory, every prisoner had volunteered to work at the mine. In fact, I never met a prisoner who had been asked whether or not he would like to become a miner. We were paid for our work, but the cost of feeding and guarding us was deducted from our earnings. These deductions were usually a little higher than, or equal to, the average miner's wages. If you did earn more than the deductions, you could buy cigarettes, crackers, or sugar.

The prisoners had come to the mine from numerous Hungarian jails and prisons, so we were all able to learn about conditions at other detention centers, the names and stories of those suffering in them, and many interesting and unique cases. These tales were told and retold, becoming more interesting and bizarre at each recounting.

Quite a few of my fellow prisoners had committed the crime of trying to leave the country. It was almost impossible to cross the Iron Curtain in those days. There were stories of ingenious but unsuccessful escape attempts. Some who tried were caught near the border; others were shot or killed by mines. Several people tried escaping by swimming downstream in the Danube to Yugoslavia, unaware of the underwater net strung across the river. Some were captured when they reached the net, and others got entangled in the net and drowned. The most famous river escapees were two acrobats. They had diving suits and tried to walk along the bottom of the river. At one place, the current became too strong and they got separated. Both swam ashore and were captured. According to the story, their case was so unusual that they were taken to Mátyás Rákosi, the dictator of Hungary. Near the time of my graduation, I also had considered escaping Hungary by swimming to Yugoslavia. One weekend I tried to swim six miles (10 km) downstream in the Danube. The water was so cold that I had to come ashore several times to get warm, so I decided not to escape by swimming. After hearing these stories from fellow prisoners, I was glad I had abandoned my plan.

As had been the case at Fő Utca prison, the common criminals working at the mine observed a hierarchy. Bank robbers were at the top, rapists at the bottom. A silent, shy man named Tóth, who everyone called Totolya, was a famous bank robber and was friendly with everybody. Before robbing banks, he had been a blacksmith. He was caught more than once but managed to escape every time. After one escape, he hid in a forest where he constructed a forge and made his own burglary tools. But his luck soon ran out. The jewelry shop he tried to break into had an alarm, so he was caught again and locked up in Fő Utca prison, where he was given work in a storeroom. One day he and another prisoner got their hands on the warden's training clothes, changed into them, climbed out a window, and started running as if in a race. They even greeted the warden, who was guarding one of the entrances, as they passed him. At least this is how Totolya told the story.

Another noteworthy character was M, a tall, strong man. He too managed to escape from a prison. Once free, he moved to Sztálinváros (Stalin City), formerly the small town of Dunapentele, but now Hungary's giant, new iron and steel works. Hungary had neither the iron ore nor the good-quality coal needed for the blast furnaces and smelters. But Stalin wanted steel works in every one of the satellite countries as a sign of progress, regardless of whether it made economic sense. The iron works needed workers and accepted anyone who applied for work, no questions asked. M started working there. Soon he met other like-minded criminals, and they developed an ingenious ruse.

At that time in Hungary, shopping at stores involved several stages. First, you had to select the items to be purchased. A cashier added up the prices of the items, printed the total, and gave a copy to the shopper. The shopper then had to pay at a second cashier, usually located far from the first group of cashiers. With the receipt marked as paid, the shopper returned to the first cashier to pick up his or her purchases. M and his companions selected two sets of merchandise. One contained several expensive items, such as TV sets, good-quality clothing and shoes, and the like. The second set consisted of cheap trinkets. For the scam to work, the total price of the trinkets had to be the same as the last three or four digits on the receipt for the expensive items. For example, if the slip for the expensive items showed 8723.45, the trinkets had to cost 23.45. One of the criminals would pay the 23.45 bill. Then, using numbers carved from hard rubber by hand, they would print 87 in front of the 23.45 on the "paid" slip. They managed to find the same ink used in the store's printers. Finally, another member of the team would pick up the expensive items with the modified receipt. They would then sell these items through a fence on the black market. They lived very well for a while. But one evening, they missed the last ferry and were left standing with all their ill-gotten goods at the terminal. A policeman asked for identification, and that was the end of their good life. In my group, M proved to be an excellent electrician, able to solve the most difficult problems in our obsolete mine. He was also the leader of the group that escaped one night through a ventilation shaft.

There were also Gypsies (Roma, the most widely accepted term in use today, was not yet common) among us, most of them condemned for some petty crime. Many of them did not even pretend to work, and I noticed that the wardens who patrolled the shafts to check if we were doing our jobs let them do nothing. They had long ago given up trying to persuade them to work.

A New Job

A FEW WEEKS after I arrived at the mine, Imre Surányi was set free. He recommended that I be named his successor in charge of the mine's machinery and electrical equipment. I moved into the barracks that housed the prisoner doctors, mining engineer, and cooks. The beds were more comfortable, and I started working in an office with the prisoner engineer. I had a staff of about a dozen electricians and a group of mechanics. I could go down to the mine anytime I found it necessary and stay there as long as I wanted.

I spent the first days in my new job studying about mining and mining machinery. Then I took a tour of the mine's machinery. I found appalling conditions. All the equipment was old and poorly maintained. The plain bearings of the conveyor belts were the worst. Years must have passed since they had last been lubricated. In more than one bearing, the axle had cut completely through the soft-bearing metal rings, the bronze bushings holding the bearing metal ring, and most of the cast-iron housing. In one of the bearings, only a very thin—less than one-eighth inch (about 3 mm)—layer of the cast-iron housing remained to hold the axle in place. This cast-iron layer was now so thin that it could rupture at any moment, causing the conveyor belt to buckle, injuring anyone standing nearby.

The mine was unable to operate at better than 20 to 40 percent efficiency. When the electrical system worked, one of the conveyor belts would break down. By the time the belt was fixed, some other piece of machinery had stopped operating. When the electrical system went out, all the machinery would stop. This happened almost every day.

I submitted a report warning about potential dangers and asking for immediate replacement of parts that could not be repaired. I repeated these requests weekly and never got an answer. I don't know if anyone ever read any of my reports.

One of my duties was to check that the wooden beams holding up the shafts and all the other reusable equipment were removed from a shaft before it was abandoned. Once the supporting beams were removed, the shaft would slowly collapse.

One long shaft had been abandoned just before Christmas. On Christmas Eve, I crawled into the half-collapsed shaft to see if anything valuable had been left there. Without ventilation, the oxygen concentration in the shaft dropped below the level necessary to keep a flame burning and soon my acetylene lamp died. It was completely dark. Just at that moment, I heard a rumbling noise and the shaft collapsed on my back. I was stuck. I realized that within minutes I would run out of oxygen. I also realized that the subsequent settling of the rocks would crush me. I did not want to die, certainly not on Christmas Eve. I immediately started to crawl backward. It is not easy to crawl backward, especially when you are stuck. I became afraid that I would never get out alive. After what felt like hours, but most likely was only minutes, I was out of the collapsing shaft. I relit my lamp and went back to the surface.

CHAPTER TWELVE

The Pear (1953–54)

NOVEMBER 25, 1953, was an important day in Hungary's soccer history. The Hungarian team played against undefeated Britain. The contest was of such magnitude to Hungary that the wardens allowed anyone not working in the mine to listen to the game on the prison camp's loudspeakers—loudspeakers that were otherwise used to broadcast important announcements, boring Communist propaganda, or music. The Hungarian team beat the British 6 to 3. The game had just ended when one of the wardens ordered me and two others to report to the main office, where we were told we were to depart for Budapest at once. We were handcuffed to one another and two wardens escorted us to the train station, where the five of us boarded the night train.

The train was full of workers and farmers. We prisoners could see the sympathy in their eyes. Many of them asked the wardens for permission to offer us cigarettes, and the wardens reluctantly agreed. This show of universal sympathy was very touching and, seeing that we were not viewed as outcasts, gave us strength to survive. It also showed that whatever support the Communists may have had among the workers and peasants in the past had vanished by 1953.

Early in the morning, the train's engine derailed. We had to wait for hours while the engine was removed, the tracks repaired, and a replacement engine installed. It was almost noon when we arrived at a suburban station in Budapest.

(Prisoners were never taken to any of the city's three main stations.) We got off the train and went to a waiting room. One of the wardens phoned to arrange transportation to our final destination. The other warden and we three prisoners sat down on the closest bench. After a sleepless night, we were very tired and promptly fell asleep.

I was half-asleep when I felt someone touching my right hand. I opened my eyes and saw a middle-aged woman in a trench coat sitting next to me. She placed something in my hand and whispered: "I'm giving you this as if you were my husband." And before I could thank her, she disappeared. In my hands was a large pear. No pear had ever tasted better.

It was late afternoon when a windowless black van finally came for us. We went to the Military Courthouse, which was housed in the same building as the Fő Utca prison. The courthouse was empty, and no one appeared to tell our wardens where to take us. Somebody finally told them to return us to Szuhakálló. We never found out why we had gone to Budapest. Most probably, we were slated to give testimony at someone else's trial. But that is just a guess.

Back at Szuhakálló

THE MINING AUTHORITIES had started a school to educate prisoners to become certified miners, and I taught classes in mining machinery and electrical equipment. At the end of the course, the students had to take exams, and those who passed received a certificate. It meant that once they were free, they would be able to work in one of the best-paying jobs available in Hungary at that time. Not surprisingly, this opportunity was very popular. The final examinations were in front of a committee, and I still remember one episode. The student was asked, "You doubtless observed that when an ax hits a rock instead of the coal, it makes sparks. How do we avoid explosions in mines containing methane gas?" After some thinking, the would-be miner answered, "Use rubber-tipped axes." He was surprised when everybody on the committee burst out laughing. The correct answer was that because the sparks emitted by the ax are cold sparks, they would not set off a methane explosion.

One morning, I was called to the gate, where I was told that a mining specialist from Budapest wanted to talk to me. I was surprised and very happy to find out that the mining specialist was my uncle Feri bácsi. He had made the journey solely to visit me—a trip that was not without risk. He would get into serious trouble if it were discovered that he used his official tour to visit an imprisoned relative. Feri bácsi and I spent the whole day together, during which he told me about how his family was doing, how many of my other relatives and friends were doing, and about the political situation in the country. I will never forget Feri bácsi's bravery and kindness.

One Saturday afternoon, two of the electricians I supervised reported a serious electrical emergency in the mine. They told me that they needed a third electrician, one especially good at fixing this type of problem. The requested electrician was assigned to a different shift, however, and my authorization was needed for him to descend into the mine a second time on the same day. I authorized his work. Overnight, the three escaped through a ventilation shaft. They had befriended a civilian electrician who removed the bars covering the shaft so they could crawl out. Their friend had also cut all the telephone lines around the mine. Then he waited in his car for the escapees to arrive. I later learned that the two on-duty electricians deliberately created the "serious electrical emergency" to create the need for the third one to help them. The wardens discovered the escape the next morning but were unable to report it until the phone lines were repaired.

None of the three escapees was a political prisoner. They were serving time for crimes like robbery or theft. Once free, they needed money, and because their criminal past precluded them from getting jobs, they resumed their old ways. All three were caught within a few months.

The following week, a couple of secret police officers arrived from Budapest. They interrogated everyone who might have assisted the three escapees or had known about their plans. Since I had authorized the third electrician to descend into the mine and join the other two, they made me responsible for the group escape. I was relieved of my position and had to work as a miner again. This meant leaving the spacious barracks for engineers, doctors, and cooks and moving back into the crowded regular barracks.

Back in the mine, I worked as helper to a civilian professional miner. One day, he needed to drill a hole to insert dynamite into the coal wall, so he sent me to get a drill from the foreman. When the hole was deep enough, he called the civilian professional miner in charge of explosives. He placed the dynamite and set off the explosion. Our shift ended shortly after the explosion, and my boss sent me to return the drill. I searched everywhere for the foreman, but before I could find him, I ran into two wardens. When they saw me carrying a drill, they accused me of trying to escape through a hole, a ridiculous accusation since it would have been impossible to dig a large enough hole with that drill.

For my punishment, I was shut into an unheated concrete cell for a few days. It already held another prisoner, who was bored and welcomed the company. He was the assistant of the famous miller of Rajka who had smuggled Hungarians into Austria and who had been captured and executed the previous year (see chapter eight). He told me about life in

Austria and Switzerland and about the movies he saw there. *The Third Man* with Orson Welles was his favorite. He also explained more specifically why he had not been executed. Although he had been born in a Hungarian-inhabited part of Slovakia, he was a Czechoslovak citizen, which saved him. He added some new details to what I already knew about that fateful final smuggling expedition with the miller, as well. A day or so before the trip, they had gone together to visit a psychic in Vienna who told the future by summoning up her deceased daughter. During the séance, the daughter's ghost had warned the two men not to return to Hungary this time. They ignored her warnings, and as I related earlier, the two of them and all of the would-be escapees were caught when the secret police intercepted a phone call that revealed the plan.

Because of poor dental care, one of my teeth had become infected. It was very painful, and the swelling distorted my face. One day, a supervisor of prison mines came to Szuhakálló to investigate the mine's poor performance. The inmates were assembled to hear his pep talk. He scolded us and ordered us to improve our output or there would be consequences. Then he looked at me and asked why I dared to laugh. I answered that I was not laughing, but that a tooth infection had distorted my face. He became very angry that I dared to contradict him, and I was immediately led back to the cold concrete cell.

Soon after that, I was transferred to the Kőbányai Gyüjtő-fogház prison near Budapest and was put in solitary confinement. One day, I heard some noise outside. Standing on my bunk, I was able to peer out the tiny cell window. A group of prisoners were walking in a circle in a small courtyard. One of them was Captain László Lepsényi, one of our commanders at the Gábor Áron military school in Nagyvárad. After the war, he continued his military service and was stationed somewhere in southwestern Hungary. When Stalin broke off with Tito, many Hungarian politicians and military officers were accused of being Titoists and arrested. Captain Lepsényi was charged with being involved with Minister of the Interior László Rajk in this conspiracy and was sentenced to hang for his role in the Rajk affair. I was surprised and happy to see him alive.

Due to nutrient-poor food and a lack of sunshine, boils plagued me and many other prisoners. One morning, I went on sick call. A large group of ailing prisoners was led single file to see a doctor. An elderly gentlemen standing next to me told me his name was Antal and that he had been a cabinet minister during the war. When I got to the doctor, I told him that I had boils. He broke off a piece of fresh yeast from a large block and told me to eat it at once. Back in my cell, I ate it. The next day, my boils were gone.

Coal Mine at Várpalota

A FEW DAYS later, I was transported to a coal mine near Várpalota. The warden on duty, Szekeres Úr (Sir Szekeres), lined up the new arrivals. He asked each of us what we had done before getting arrested. Most of the prisoners responded that they were farmers. When I told him that I was a chemical engineer, he shouted, "I hate you because I hate everybody who is like a teacher. I assure you, you'll have a very difficult life here!" Indeed, he did everything to make my life as miserable as possible.

Várpalota mine was in the eastern slopes of the Bakony Mountains, about forty-four miles (70 km) southwest of Budapest. The mine, which was much bigger than the one at Szuhakálló, harbored more than eleven hundred prisoners, and its seam of lignite was thick. Lignite is young brown coal, intermediate between peat and subbituminous coal, and because it is wet, it must be dried before it can be used. Its flame is long and smoky, and its heating power is low. The mining equipment at Várpalota was in good shape, and every piece of machinery worked all the time. Miners who produced more coal than the norm were rewarded. Each percent above 100 percent of a miner's output was equated to a specified number of days off the miner's sentence. The performance of many miners could not be expressed in percentages, however, so they were rewarded according to the average performance of the mine. As a result, all the prisoners worked as hard as possible, and the mine's monthly average was well above 100 percent during my time there.

The mine entrance was more than an hour away from the miners' barracks. The Communist government introduced a "hot ax shift rotation," that is, one shift could stop working only when the next shift was ready to take over. Thus, nearly two hours of free time were lost walking to work and then back to our barracks. That also meant that the afternoon shift had to eat lunch about three hours before the morning crew finished work. Lunch was usually kept warm for the morning workers. One hot summer day a pasta dish spoiled. The next day, almost everyone on the morning shift was ill.

Standard practice was to mine the coal from only one layer, wait several years for the earth to settle, and then mine the other layer. One not-too-brilliant top Communist leader decided to increase production by mining from the second layer right after all the coal from the first layer was removed. Some of the unsettled shafts caved in and others flooded. Several miners perished in these senseless accidents.

Most of the time, I worked with another prisoner filling trolleys from a conveyor belt, pushing the trolleys to the main shaft, and then coupling them there to the cable that pulled them to the surface. The other prisoner was a very strong man from the Bácska, a part of Hungary that was attached to Yugoslavia at the end of World War I. He had escaped from Yugoslavia to Hungary, and instead of giving him the asylum he requested, the Hungarian secret police incarcerated him. He was a very nice man, and we became good friends.

I spent most of my free time in the open, enjoying the sunshine. I borrowed a physical chemistry book from another prisoner and read it from cover to cover.

All of our mail was handled by older or handicapped prisoners and was censored. One day, I received my Stakhanovite certificate from the Forte factory. I had been named a Stakhanovite because I had discovered the structure of a new film stabilizer and developed a process to manufacture it (see chapter five). When the mail handlers saw my certificate, they warned all the prisoners that because I was a Stakhanovite, I must be a Communist and should be avoided. The irony of this was that the people at Forte had sent the certificate with the thought that it would ease my situation.

On the afternoon of June 30, I was called to the warden's office. I was being released before completing my fourteen-month sentence. I got three weeks off due to the mine's high average performance.

I exchanged my striped prisoner suit for some horrible-looking civilian clothes, signed a paper promising to return the clothes by mail as soon as I arrived in Budapest, got some pocket money, and walked out of the prison camp. I was free! I hurried to the Várpalota railroad station, where I discovered there was more than an hour's wait before the next train to Budapest. So I sat in a pastry shop and ate several slices of *dobos torta* and *krémes* and drank an espresso.

The train ride to Budapest was interesting. First, there was a partial solar eclipse. Second, one of the crucial soccer matches of the World Cup was going on that afternoon, with the Hungarian team playing Uruguay. Stationmasters at each stop put radios near the rails so passengers could follow the progress of the game for a few minutes. Improvised boards displayed the score at stations where the train did not stop. Hungary won!

Thirty-seven years later, on October 1, 1991, the Military Court of Budapest invalidated my sentence that had been upheld by the appeals court on October 21, 1953. Captain Béla Varga, judge of the Military Court of Budapest, signed the Nullity Resolution on that day.[18] And on February 15, 1994, a Hungarian military court rehabilitated me with the rank of retired *zászlós* (ensign).

CHAPTER THIRTEEN

Free Again (1954–56)

THE FIRST THING I had to do in Budapest was to report my release at an army office, where a young officer handled the relevant document. He asked me whether he should discharge me or if I preferred to go back to my forced labor battalion. I answered that I would like a discharge. He looked at me, smiled, and wrote "Discharged" on the document. I thanked him, we shook hands, and I left. Now I was really free. But I had no place to live. Fortunately, the parents of my best friend, György Szabó, offered me a room until I could find more permanent lodgings.

My second task was to return the civilian clothes I had been issued for the train ride to Budapest. I mailed the clothes back the next morning.

All around me people were talking about Hungary's chances of winning the World Cup. The final game was between Hungary and Germany. This was a bit strange because Hungary had already played the Germans and beat them. Everybody expected the Hungarian team to win again, of course. But Mátyás Rákosi, the party secretary, wanted the team to have Communist players and replaced some of the best players with Communists. When the Germans beat this politically reconfigured team, a wave of protests erupted. Some estimates put the number of protesters in Budapest above a hundred thousand. The crowd plundered the coach's house, and the returning players were taken off the train at a small station west of Budapest and secretly smuggled to their homes in the city.

Budapest had a shortage of apartments. The long siege during the winter of 1944–45 had resulted in the destruction of thousands of buildings. The Communists occupied themselves with erecting statues and other monuments glorifying Communism and building luxury homes for top party functionaries, but they constructed very few homes for the general population. Almost every apartment housed two or more families, which made it hard for me to find a place to live.

I finally found a room on Mártirok útja (now Margit Boulevard) in an apartment owned by Lipcsey Ádám bácsi and his sister, Teca néni. A nice, young couple occupied the second large room, formerly the dining room when only one family had resided there. An old lady lived in what had been the maid's room. There was one kitchen and one bathroom. The room I rented had once been a walk-in closet, and its only window opened on a narrow ventilation shaft. This window, when open, let in some fresh air but almost no light. I had to turn on the light even on a sunny day. The room had no stove or other heat source, and there was just enough room for a bed, a wardrobe, and a small desk. My housemates, however, were very pleasant. Such harmonious living conditions were rare when several families were forced to share the same apartment, including a single kitchen and bathroom. I really liked Ádám bácsi and Teca néni, and I stayed in contact with them until the end of their lives. Following the collapse of the 1956 revolution, food shortages were common in Hungary. I tried to ease their hardship by sending them several food packages.

After a few days in Budapest, I went to Balatonszemes to rest, swim, and enjoy my freedom. But I could not stay long. Because I was on probation for fourteen months, I was required to report to the police before the end of July that I had secured a permanent job, so I went back to Budapest and started searching for employment. First I tried the NEVIKI research institute in Veszprém, the last place I worked before I was drafted into forced labor. My application was denied. The party secretary did not want a former political prisoner working at his prestigious institute.

I tried several chemical factories and research laboratories. At every place, the engineer who interviewed me would have been happy to employ me. I was introduced to the technical directors, and they, too, were always positive. Each time they told me that I should come back the next morning for the final answer. But when I returned as instructed, I was always told that, regretfully, they could not hire me. At almost every place, one of the chemists quietly let me know that the institution's Communist Party secretary objected to hiring an ex-felon convicted of a political crime.

I was getting desperate. If I could not find a job soon, I would have to go back to prison. Fortunately, one of Béla bácsi's friends found me a job at Tükert, a coal distribution company. I was once again shoveling coal all day, just as I had at Várpalota. But now I was shoveling it in bright sunlight.

On my second day of work, on my way home, I met my friend Tibor Wein, a chemical engineer. He was the head of a department at the Kőbányai Gyógyszerárugyár, a large pharmaceutical factory. He promised to arrange a better job for me and told me to come and see him in two days' time.

When I asked my boss if I could start a few hours later on the following day, he said I could not. I decided that if I really could get a job at the pharmaceutical factory, it was worth the risk, so I quit.

I reported for an interview the following morning at Kőbányai Gyógyszerárugyár. Tibor told me that I would work in his department (Kémia V), and that I would be hired as a worker but would work as an engineer. My desk would be in a room with the other engineers, and I would have my own projects and a staff of three assistants. Because my official status was worker and not engineer, the Communist Party did not oppose this arrangement. I started the next day.

Work at Kőbányai Gyógyszerárugyár

THE PHARMACIST GEDEON Richter had established the Richter Gedeon Gyógyszerárugyár in 1901, the first pharmaceutical factory in Hungary. During World War II, the plant suffered heavy damage, and Gedeon Richter was killed by the Nazis. In 1948, the Communist government nationalized the plant, taking it away from Richter's heirs, and renamed it the Kőbányai Gyógyszerárugyár (Kőbánya Pharmaceutical Factory). The company continued to use the Gedeon Richter, Ltd. name in foreign markets. It ranked among the largest suppliers in the world of vitamin B_{12} and several other drugs. At that time, it was Hungary's second largest pharmaceutical factory.

I soon learned the advantages of being a worker and not an engineer. The Kémia V department had two responsibilities: developing new processes and manufacturing low volume (that is, less than two hundred kilograms per month) pharmaceuticals.

Many of the processes were obsolete. Products often did not meet purity requirements. Unlike the chemists and engineers in charge of improving processes, workers were rewarded for whatever innovations they made. The reward was 1 percent of what that particular innovation saved in the year following its introduction. The professionals were not rewarded because it was their job to improve obsolete or imperfect processes. They were rewarded only if an improvement generated a new patent, though rewards for patents were substantially larger. My base salary was less than that of a starting engineer, but I soon started to earn more than most of the engineers in our department through my innovations. I could buy better food and the books I wanted, afford good seats at the opera and theater, spend every summer weekend in Balatonszemes, and go to a nice restaurant once in a while. I also bought a high-quality radio and a camera. I added to my earnings by tutoring a middle-aged gentleman who needed to pass some chemistry exams to gain a promotion.

Until about 1954, the Kőbányai Gyógyszerárugyár produced pharmaceuticals mostly for Hungary and other Eastern Bloc countries. In 1954, the factory started to market in Western Europe and other countries where product-purity requirements were much higher. The company's goal was to ensure that all of its products conformed to US specifications. My major task was to improve product purity. The most interesting project was the quality improvement of the antiseptic and antifungal agent merthiolate (or thimerosal, the sodium salt of ethylmercury thiosalicylic acid). I found a new way to crystallize a final product that was much purer than what the company had been making. Ethylmercury chloride, one of the intermediate chemicals used in the synthesis, is highly toxic. It could enter the body both by inhalation and by dermal penetration, and its effects are cumulative. Soon after I started working with this compound, I noticed signs of mercury poisoning: pain in the stomach, a bad taste in my mouth, and bleeding gums. A laboratory test confirmed that my blood had an unacceptably high level of mercury. The doctor recommended the use of rubber gloves and other safety measures. I also had to eat a raw egg daily. That helped.

Then I arranged tests for my associates. The department's Communist Party functionary accused me of needlessly creating panic among the workers. After he learned that the test results for my three associates were positive, he shut up.

From then on, everyone became much more careful. Still, it took weeks to get rid of all the mercury in our bodies. Those who worked with benzene or mercury or other poisonous substances received daily doses of milk and of rose hip tea or rose hip jam, which is rich in vitamin C. Our work week grew shorter and we received more vacation than the others.

Another interesting project was the production of the hormone and neurotransmitter L-adrenaline (or epinephrine). One of its uses is to retard the spread of—and therefore prolong the action of—anesthetics such as novocaine. The plant's production of two hundred grams per month met the demand of much of the Eastern Bloc. Its synthesis had many steps and the purity requirements were stringent. That made the product very expensive. I produced several "improvements" and one patent covering process modifications.

Reconnecting with My Family

BY 1955–1956, COMMUNICATION with relatives living in the Free World was no longer forbidden. I started exchanging letters with my parents almost weekly. Most of their letters arrived unopened, or so it appeared. My parents also sent many gift packages, which always contained clothes and cosmetics. My mother was an Avon saleslady for a couple of years in Cleveland, Ohio, and could obtain the cosmetics at a discount. I gave the cosmetics to relatives and friends, or I sold them on the black market, which boosted my income. Finally, I had decent, good-quality clothes and shoes.

I spent most of my vacation days in Balatonszemes. One day on the beach, I met a group of twenty-five Arabs who were enjoying a few days layover before returning home from the Warsaw World Youth Festival. These international festivals were organized to brainwash naïve young people. Sometimes they succeeded, and sometimes not. I asked one of the Arabs how many in the group considered themselves Communists. "When we left home, twenty-four of us were Communists and one was not," he answered. "Now there's only one Communist and twenty-four who are not."

I recall a day in 1949 when the World Youth Festival was organized in Budapest. I was headed to central Pest when a well-dressed blonde girl stopped me and asked in English if I spoke English. Before I could start to answer, two strong men grabbed me and carried me away from the girl and told me never to attempt to talk to any foreigner. The regime took every step to inhibit Westerners from learning the true nature of Communism. Apparently, even the strongest measures had failed with those Arabs. I also recall that throughout 1949, there was almost no milk, butter, or meat available in the stores. But during the World Youth Festival, the same stores were full of sausages, salami, ham, and all types of meat, cheese, butter, and the like. The day after the festival ended, all these foods disappeared again.

One day while I was out walking, I ran into the judge who had presided at my first trial in early August 1953. We sat down on a bench overlooking the Danube to talk. He told me that the appeals court should have set me free. He was very sorry when I told him that despite my objections, the day before the appeals court hearing, I was forcibly taken to work in a mine. I also told him that Sándor Ray, my court-appointed lawyer, had failed to appear at the hearing.

Since neither of us was present, the appeals court did not change the original verdict.

By this time, I had enough money to pay Comrade Ray the 1,000 forints he had charged me for his services. Because he had failed to attend my appeal hearing, I felt he did not deserve the money, but I paid him.

Love

IN LATE 1955, I met Gabi Szemere at a party in Budapest. We soon fell in love.

Gabi had been born Gabrielle Szemere on January 23, 1932, in Budapest. She had two brothers, Pali, who was two years her senior, and Miklós, who was four years her junior. She went to school in Budapest, graduating from the Roman Catholic Saint Ursula High School, and she spent most summers in Nagykökényes in Nógrád County, where her father owned six hundred *hold* (about 850 acres). The property included twenty-eight acres of orchards, a house, and a large stable for cows and horses. After World War II, the government appropriated all the land except the orchards. A few years later, the Communists classified her family as kulaks and thus "enemies of the people," which meant that every year the tax on the orchards would increase. The tax was eventually so high that Gabi's father was unable to pay it. The government's response was to imprison him for a year and to confiscate the orchards.

In June 1951, when tens of thousands of middle-class families were forcibly deported to the countryside and their homes and most of their belongings were confiscated, Gabi's family was banished to the village of Csány, in Heves County. No family member could ever leave the village, and the police checked often, usually in the middle of the night, to make sure the rule was followed. All five family members lived in a single room at a farmer's house—a fellow kulak—and they all had to work on a state farm. A few months after the family's arrival, Pali was conscripted and was taken away to work as a forced laborer in a mine for two years.

In the summer of 1953, Imre Nagy's reforms allowed the deportees to move anywhere they wished except for Budapest and some other large cities. Gabi's parents took up residence in Páty, not too far from Budapest, and Gabi went to work as a nurse's assistant in a hospital in Gyöngyös, a small city in Heves County. After a year, she got a job in the Central Dental Clinic of Budapest and soon became a dental assistant. She was not allowed to live in Budapest, however, and commuting regularly from Páty to the center of the city would have been almost impossible because of the distance. To solve the problem, she illegally rented a bed at the home of the Sztudinka family in Szentkirályi Street, which was very close to the dental clinic. The Sztudinkas were from Kassa, and Mr. Sztudinka had served with my father as a reserve officer. His eldest son was my Boy Scout patrol leader.

Gabi had to avoid being seen by the concierge when she entered and left the house, and she had to be home every night before nine o'clock, when the gate was locked. Only concierges had keys to the gates, and they were required to report all unregistered individuals entering or leaving the buildings. Twice a week, after her regular working hours at the clinic, Gabi worked at another dental office to supplement her meager income, which made her comings and goings even riskier.

My godfather, Gyula bácsi, asked Gabi's father for her hand for me. We became engaged in the late summer of 1956.

The author, age 15, in cadet uniform in the summer of 1944 (Photo by Zsigmond Csicsery)

The author holding his cousin Margit Módly while visiting his aunt Margit néni in 1952 at the farm to which her family had been deported (Photo by Béla Módly)

The author and the riverboat Szabadság *(Freedom) in 1955 (Photographer unknown; courtesy of the author)*

The author in 1956 (Courtesy
of the author)

The author in 1956 (Courtesy of the
author)

The author, January 8, 1956 (Photo
by Gabrielle Csicsery)

The author, March 4, 1956 (Photo
by Gabrielle Csicsery)

Self-portrait in the author's room on Mártirok útja, Budapest, March 26, 1956

Prédikálószék (the Pulpit), Visegrád Mountains, October 1956
(Photo by Tivadar Lehoczky)

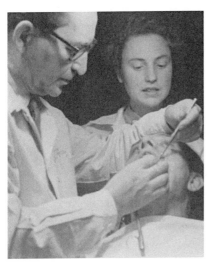

Gabi Szemere in Balatonszemes, July 15, 1956 (Photo by the author)

Gabi Szemere working as a dental assistant in Budapest, January 1956. (Photographer unknown; courtesy of Gabrielle Csicsery)

Gabi Szemere in 1956 (Photo by the author)

Gabi Szemere in Balatonszemes, July 15, 1956 (Photo by the author)

The author and Gabi Szemere with his uncle Gyula and Gyula's wife, Ella, in Fenyves, May 2, 1956 (Photo by the author)

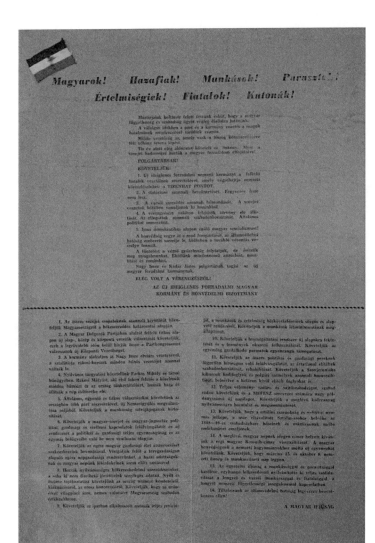

This may be one of the first versions of the sixteen points printed on October 23 or early on October 24. The author got this copy early on October 24 in Pest. He spent much of that day reading it to groups of people assembled on street corners on the Buda side. (Courtesy of the author)

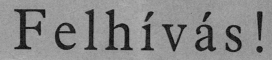

Felhívás!

1. Követeljük, hogy az ÁVH azonnal szüntesse be a harcot.

2. Követeljük, hogy a szovjet csapatok azonnal hagyják el a főváros területét.

3. Követeljük, hogy mindenkinek, akik a harcokban résztvettek amnesztiát adjanak.

4. Politikai menedékjogot adjanak azoknak a szovjet harcosoknak, akik a harcokban a munkásság mellé álltak.

5. Követeljük, hogy a magyar néphadsereg vegye át a rend fenntartását.

MŰSZAKI EGYETEM
KÖZPONTI DIÁKOTTHONA

Leaflet probably composed and printed on October 22 at the Technical University. (Courtesy of the author)

CHAPTER FOURTEEN

The Hungarian Revolution of 1956

HUNDREDS OF BOOKS have been written about the 1956 Hungarian Revolution. In this chapter, I will only summarize the events of that time and describe what I did and what I saw during those days.

In 1945, the Independent Smallholders' Party won the elections. For three years after World War II, Hungary was a multiparty democracy. However, the minority Communist Party, with the help of occupying Soviet forces, rose to power in a step-by-step process called "salami tactics." The most important step was the transfer of the Ministry of the Interior from the Independent Smallholders' Party to the Communist Party. Through false accusations, imprisonment, torture, and intimidation, the Hungarian State Security Police (Államvédelmi Osztály, known as the ÁVO, and after 1948 Államvédelmi Hatóság, known as the ÁVH) gradually eliminated all political opposition. Thousands were arrested, tortured, tried, and then imprisoned in concentration camps. Many hundreds were executed, including László Rajk, former minister of interior and founder of the ÁVH. Meanwhile the Communist Party changed the capitalist economic system to a socialist one.

As described in chapter eight, a few months after Joseph Stalin's death on March 5, 1953, the moderate Imre Nagy replaced Mátyás Rákosi as Hungary's prime minister and immediately introduced a series of reforms. But Rákosi, who remained general secretary of the Communist Party, was able to undermine most of Nagy's actions. In the spring of 1955, Rákosi and his clique expelled Nagy from the party, and it was no surprise when Rákosi again became prime minister.

At the 20th Congress of the Communist Party of the Soviet Union in February 1956, Nikita Khrushchev denounced Stalin's cult of personality. When the Kremlin's new leaders also decided to restore friendly relations with Yugoslavia's Tito, the so-called Titoists imprisoned in Hungary and in other satellite countries were released. In Hungary, these newly freed Titoists blamed Rákosi for their imprisonment and for the execution of the former interior minister László Rajk and his alleged coconspirators.

By this time, even most of those people who once believed sincerely in the promise of a bright and just Communist future were disillusioned with the system. These former Communists became the most vocal critics of the Rákosi regime. The Communist-dominated Hungarian Writers' Union was now a state within a state. Journalists and writers in the Petőfi Circle started to criticize the government openly at their meetings, especially Rákosi and his policies. The group's publication, *The Literary Gazette*, reached a circulation of 450,000 in a country of only ten million people. The writers started an independent weekly newspaper, which appeared on Mondays, but they were never allocated enough paper to meet the constantly growing demand. By the time the vendors showed up late on Sunday to pick up their allotted quota, large crowds, anxious to buy the paper, had already gathered outside the printing office. One evening, a vendor had to climb a tree to avoid being trampled by eager buyers. He sold his papers from his perch on the branches.

The collapse of Stalinism had created a political vacuum in Hungary. On October 6, 1956, Rákosi's number one victim, László Rajk, was ceremoniously reburied. Thousands attended the event. Then Imre Nagy, who had been dismissed a year earlier for his liberal policies, was rehabilitated and readmitted to the Hungarian Workers' Party, that is, the Communist Party.

For nearly a decade, everyone had to hide his or her feelings because no one knew whom to trust and who might be an informer. After Rákosi's fall, people suddenly realized that nearly everybody hated Communism, including disillusioned party members and former believers.

On October 16, 1956, students at Szeged University ended the official Communist student union, DISZ, and reestablished MEFESZ (Union of Hungarian University and Academy Students), a democratic student organization banned by the Rákosi regime. Within days, students at the universities of Pécs, Miskolc, and Sopron followed suit. On October 22, students at the Technical University of Budapest reestablished their MEFESZ student union and compiled a list of sixteen demands, which they published in a leaflet and distributed (see Appendix 1 for an English-language summary of the sixteen points).

October 23, 1956

AT ABOUT THE same time, Władysław Gomułka, a reformist Communist and the first secretary of the Polish United Workers' Party, negotiated trade concessions and troop reductions for Poland with the Soviet government. On October 19, the Soviets accepted Gomułka's demands. To express solidarity with the Polish reform movement, Hungarian students at the Technical University of Budapest organized a rally to lay a wreath at the statue of Polish-born General József Bem, a hero of the Hungarian Revolution of 1848.

I was on my way home from work when I heard about the solidarity rally. Instead of going home, I joined the students marching to Bem Square and met my cousin András among the marchers. András pinned a miniature Hungarian flag—a red, white, and green cockade that I still have—on my jacket.

The gathering turned into a mass demonstration calling for Hungary's independence from Moscow's control. Civilians and a group of soldiers from a nearby barracks joined our rally. One officer asked for silence and then read a poem he had composed to celebrate Polish-Hungarian friendship. When someone in the crowd asked him why he had a red star on his cap, he tore it off. The crowd applauded, and many of the soldiers followed his example. Then someone produced a Hungarian tricolor flag. At that time, the flag had a Communist emblem, similar to the Russian hammer and sickle, at its center. The man cut this symbol out of the flag. These flags with a circular hole at their center became the symbols of our revolution.

According to some estimates, about twenty thousand protesters had gathered at the Bem statue. We now marched across the Danube to Parliament Square to present our demands to the government. We chanted "Ruszkik haza!" (Russians go home!) and other slogans for freedom and independence. People all around us showed their support, cheering from the sidewalks and windows. By six o'clock, the multitude in front of Parliament had increased to over two hundred thousand people.

The crowd wanted to hear Imre Nagy. As we waited, tens of thousands more people swelled our ranks. It was growing late and had started to get dark. Finally, Imre Nagy appeared on one of the building's balconies. Apparently, he did not yet realize that we were there to demand an end to Soviet rule and Communism, as he addressed us as comrades.

At eight o'clock, the hardliner first secretary of the Hungarian Communist Party, Ernő Gerő, made an unscheduled radio announcement. He condemned the demands of the writers and students. He also dispelled the "lies and rumors" that Hungary wanted to loosen its ties with the Soviet Union. The demonstrators considered Gerő's speech an insult.

In 1951, the Communists had erected a huge bronze statue of Joseph Stalin alongside Városliget, a large park near the center of Budapest. A Roman Catholic church had been demolished to make room for sculptor Sándor Mikus's work, which stood thirty feet (9 m) high atop a thirteen-foot (4-m) limestone pedestal that rested on a large tribune. The statue symbolized both the hated Communist system and the Soviet occupation, so some of us gathered at the Parliament decided to pull it down. As we started walking toward it, a few empty trucks rolled by. I jumped in front of the first one and waved it to a stop. The driver asked what I wanted, and I told him that we were on our way to pull down Stalin's statue and would he be so nice as to take us there. Without a word, he stepped on his accelerator and drove away. But after a short distance, he stopped, turned around, and motioned for us to board. We filled his truck within seconds. Other trucks followed our driver's example, and our convoy started moving toward the statue. Whenever we passed a streetcar or a bus, our driver slowed down to match the streetcar's speed and we chanted, "Ledőntjük a Sztálin szobrot!" (We are going to topple the Stalin statue!) At first the passengers looked away as if they did not hear our sacrilegious words. But each time, after a few seconds, they turned around and joined our chanting. Some of the buses changed direction and joined our ever-expanding convoy. And when the streetcars stopped, most of the passengers got off and proceeded on foot toward the statue.

By the time we arrived at the statue, the large square in front of it was already full of people. Some athletic young men were on top of the statue busily affixing steel cables around Stalin's neck. The men tied the other ends of the cables to trucks. But when the trucks started to pull, the cables snapped. Many people, including me, shouted to bring acetylene torches to cut the statue's ankles. Soon some torches, oxygen cylinders, and metal-cutting blowpipes arrived, and a small group of expert workmen started to cut the bronze boots. However, the base of the statue was filled with concrete almost to its knees, so the workmen had to make a second cut higher up and affix new steel cables around the statue's neck. This time, twice as many trucks moved into position to pull at the cables, and each truck was boarded by as many people as possible to increase its weight and thus gain better traction. The crowd grew quiet when the trucks were ready, then all the trucks started pulling at once. Minutes passed without anything happening. But suddenly the enormous statue began slowly leaning forward. Finally, with a tremendous roar, the statue went crashing to the pavement.

For a few seconds, it was absolutely quiet. Then, without any suggestion or order, we all started singing the Hungarian national anthem, "Isten áldd meg a magyart" ("God, Bless the Hungarians"). This was the happiest moment of my life.

According to estimates, the crowd now numbered over one hundred thousand. People ran to the fallen statue, jumped on it, trampled it for a few minutes, and then stepped back to let others take their turn at trampling this symbol of tyranny. Later that night, Stalin's head was severed, pulled to a prominent site in Pest, and left there so everybody could enjoy seeing it. During the following days, people cut or hammered small pieces of the bronze to keep as souvenirs. One of Stalin's hands was hidden in a garden. Today it is in a museum.

A few minutes before the statue came down, a man had climbed up on its base and announced that another large crowd had gathered at the Budapest Radio building. A student delegation had entered the building to ask the radio to broadcast their demands—the sixteen points. The ÁVH detachment guarding the building then detained them. The crowd demanded their release to no avail. A rumor that the ÁVH had shot the detainees began to spread. When the crowd grew noisier, the ÁVH threw tear gas and shot at the crowd, killing many. The man bringing this news suggested that after we pulled down the statue, we should go to the radio building. And so we did.

As I approached Sándor Street and the radio building, I heard sporadic gunshots. My fiancée Gabi's apartment on Szentkirályi Street stood next to the building. I had to circle around the block to avoid Sándor Street, where the ÁVH were shooting anyone they could see. Although a small group of city policemen stood at the gate, I had no problem getting into Gabi's building. Mrs. Sztudinka opened the door and told me that Gabi was hiding in the bathroom. Gabi was happy to see me. Just a few minutes earlier, she had spat on the policemen from the window above the entrance, and when she heard the doorbell, she thought it was the police coming to get her.

I left to rejoin the protesters. The ÁVH unit guarding the radio building had tried to resupply itself by ferrying arms inside ambulance cars. Some demonstrators had discovered this and armed themselves with the weapons meant to reinforce the ÁVH.

The hard-line Hungarian Communist leadership probably thought that the secret police units would easily deal with the student demonstration and restore order. They must have been surprised when, by nightfall, thousands of workers had joined the students. The government then ordered regular army units from nearby barracks to relieve the besieged ÁVH troops. But the army units ordered to fight us switched sides and joined us.

I went to the Astoria restaurant at the corner of Kossuth Lajos Street and Múzeum Ring Road, at the center of Pest. Regular army units were lined up along the north side of Kossuth Lajos Street. It was obvious these soldiers were sympathetic to our cause. They hated the ÁVH just as much as we did. Demonstrators were talking to the officers everywhere, asking for their weapons. A young officer next to me asked how we could imagine that a soldier—any soldier—would ever give his weapon to civilians.

"Under what circumstances would you give us your weapons?" one of us asked the officer.

"Only in a case of overwhelming force," the officer answered.

"And what would you consider overwhelming force?" was the next question.

The officer answered, "If you say that you will use force, I would consider that to be enough." And then he asked, "Now, do you know how to use a submachine gun?"

The officer promptly gave us a brief lecture on how to operate a submachine gun and then ordered his men to give us theirs. There were many of us and only a small number of guns, so all I got was ammunition.

It was late and I was getting tired. I dropped in on some friends nearby, but after a short rest, I decided to go back to Gabi's place. A distant relative named Hámos joined me. But we couldn't even get close to Gabi's place. As we turned onto Szentkirályi Street, an ÁVH marksman shot at us. A dead body already lay on the street right in front of us. We jumped into a doorway, joining a crowd of people taking cover there. At about 2 a.m., the apartment building's concierge came to tell us that he had heard on the radio that Ernő Gerő had asked for Soviet military intervention after learning the army had sided with the demonstrators. An armored division of Soviet forces stationed at Székesfehérvár was already on its way to Budapest. The concierge assumed that should Russian soldiers discover demonstrators under the doorway of his building, they would kill everyone living there. We understood his request. Indeed, shortly after 2 a.m., the first Soviet tanks entered Budapest.

We had to leave. The lone streetlight provided just enough light for the ÁVH marksman across the street to shoot anyone trying to step outside the gate. We had to get rid of the street lamp. It hung on a wire barely sixty-five feet (20 m) away. We took turns trying to hit the lamp with the only gun we had. We wasted about forty shots before a bullet finally knocked out the light.

We could now leave safely under cover of darkness. Hámos and I went to the building where Gabi lived. On the way to the second floor, we passed by a window overlooking the courtyard of the radio building. A young man with a gun stood at the window, covering the back entrance to the building. I gave him all the ammunition I had been carrying with me.

From the window of the Sztudinkas' apartment, we watched the last of the ÁVH men surrender to a few young men armed with submachine guns. The radio building was now ours. But our joy was premature. The Communists had another radio center hidden somewhere inside a hill, so they were able to continue broadcasting. They announced that the fights in Sándor Street were over and that the radio station was in government hands. Gabi and I decided to walk around the city and tell everyone we met that this was not true and that we had witnessed the fall of the radio building. We crossed the Danube to the Buda side to continue spreading this message. At one point, through an open window, we heard that the government had ordered an immediate curfew. The consequence of this announcement was astonishing: gates opened everywhere and the streets filled with people.

October 25, 1956—Bloody Thursday

ON THE MORNING of October 25, tens of thousands of protesters gathered in front of the Parliament building. They were demanding that former prime minister Imre Nagy be returned to power. This peaceful demonstration soon turned into a notorious massacre that became known as Bloody Thursday. According to some observers, the carnage started when ÁVH units provoked nearby Soviet troops by shooting toward them from the rooftops of neighboring buildings. Others said the ÁVH began firing at the demonstrators, and then some Soviet soldiers, mistakenly believing that they were the targets, started shooting into the crowd. Before long, Soviet tanks opened fire on the crowd at point-blank range. Within minutes, Parliament Square was littered with hundreds of dead and thousands of wounded people.

An hour before the shooting started, Gabi and I and György Szabó, my best friend, and his wife, Zsuzsa, together with hundreds of other would-be demonstrators, had set out to join the gathering multitude at Parliament Square. We had almost reached the Pest side of Margaret Bridge when we heard the first shots. We were no more than a few hundred meters from Jászai Mari Square and ÁVH headquarters, and the gunfire sounded as if the bullets were coming toward us from the roof of the ÁVH building. We turned around and ran to the center of the bridge, where the walls of a pedestrian walkway that led to Margaret Island offered good protection.

When the shooting stopped, we left the bridge, but instead of going back to Buda, we proceeded north along the protected west side of Margaret Island. At the north end of the island, we returned to Buda by way of another bridge. Once back on the Buda side, we turned south, moving toward where both the Szabós and I lived. At one point, we passed a building with a large, five-pointed red star above its gate, a sure sign that it was an office of the ÁVH or the Communist Party. A small group was gathered near the entrance, where they were contemplating how to remove the star. When we got there, Gyuri and I clasped our hands to create a platform for a tall man to stand on and reach the star. Just as he was about to pull it down, the doors of the building opened. Two ÁVH men appeared and pushed the barrels of their submachine guns into my and Gyuri's chests. Because the man was standing on our hands, Gyuri and I couldn't move. But the man knew what to do. He jumped on the two ÁVH men and shouted, "Don't do anything crazy!" and pushed them back into the doorway.

We expected the ÁVH men to return with reinforcements and kill us. Our small group dispersed at once, with the Szabós, Gabi, and I fleeing into a nearby café. One of the waitresses turned out to be the sister of a lady who lived in the apartment where I lived. I told her what had happened, and she led us to a back door. We followed her directions and returned safely to Gyuri's home. I later learned that a group of armed freedom fighters captured the building without meeting any resistance. All of the ÁVH men had fled before they arrived.

Meanwhile, the carnage at Parliament Square continued. The Russians even shot ambulance workers trying to remove the wounded. The exact number of casualties is unknown. The ÁVH hauled away some of the dead. According to one rumor, some of the fallen were entombed in concrete in the ÁVH barracks on Kerepesi Road. Only 234 of the dead were ever identified.

In a Radio Kossuth broadcast at three o'clock that same day, Imre Nagy said, "Every drop of blood of those innocent workingmen who fell during these tragic days fills me with deep sorrow." (Mélységes fájdalommal tölt el e tragikus napok során áldozatul esett ártatlan dolgozó emberek minden csepp kiömlött vére.)

On October 25, Hungary's Communist government collapsed. First Secretary Ernő Gerő, former prime minister András Hegedüs, and a handful of other leaders fled to the Soviet Union. The new government included some non-Communist ministers. Imre Nagy became prime minister. He called our activities "a broad democratic mass movement."

Soviet tanks remained on the streets for a few more days while the uprising continued. Impromptu councils took over municipal control from the Communist Party and demanded political changes. An armored division of the Hungarian army commanded by Pál Maléter chose to join the freedom fighters rather than defend the Communists. Activities of the Soviets in Budapest were eventually brought to a standstill. A ceasefire was arranged on October 28, and by October 30, most of the Soviet troops had withdrawn from the city. The new government disbanded the ÁVH, abolished the one-party system, promised free elections, and stated its desire to withdraw from the Warsaw Pact. The spontaneously formed Revolutionary Workers' Councils and national committees started to develop the process of democratic self-determination.

A few days later, a crowd assembled in front of the Communist Party central headquarters at Republic Square to search for children the ÁVH might have arrested as hostages. The people demanded entry. When the ÁVH refused their request, members of the crowd lynched several ÁVH officers. During the uprising, many reporters noted the surprising absence of violence and looting by the protestors, with this the only major atrocity committed by the freedom fighters. *Life* photographer John Sadovy captured the horror of these lynchings, and his photographs were widely published throughout the West.

At Republic Square, some people said they heard sounds emanating from underground, which they suspected came from secret ÁVH prisons in the cellars. Several days of digging with bulldozers revealed nothing. Then the radio announced an appeal for anyone with knowledge about the cellars under the building to come forward. Most likely, there were no secret jails or cellars there.

On October 30, Soviet troops withdrew from Budapest. Revolutionary councils replaced the triumvirates that had managed every enterprise: the Communist Party secretary, the head of the company, and the personnel director. One of the first actions of these new councils was the release of the hated secret dossiers on employees that were kept in every personnel office.

For a few days, Hungary was free.

Defeat

The glorious days of victory ended in deceit and a brutal attack by overwhelming Soviet forces.

The Soviet invasion coincided with a war in the Middle East. Egypt's leader, Gamal Abdel Nasser, had decided to take over the Suez Canal. England, France, and Israel promptly attacked Egypt. The Soviet Union objected and offered armed help to Nasser. The United States requested that England, France, and Israel withdraw their troops immediately to avoid Soviet intervention.

The Suez Crisis diverted attention from Hungary. It was also unfortunate that our revolution coincided with the US presidential elections and with the postsurgery hospitalization of Secretary of State John Foster Dulles, who had been against British and French involvement in the Suez Crisis. According to some sources, China's leader, Mao Zedong, strongly encouraged Khrushchev to suppress the Hungarian uprising.

At first, the Soviet Politburo announced a willingness to negotiate the withdrawal of Soviet forces from Hungary. It invited Pál Maléter, Hungary's new minister of defense, to negotiations in Tököl, a town close to Budapest. At about midnight, General Ivan Serov, chief of the KGB, arrested the Hungarian delegation. Then, in the early hours of November 4, the Soviet army invaded Hungary with about five thousand tanks, many planes, and fresh troops. They encircled Budapest and moved in to crush the revolution. A large fleet of tanks entered the city and armored units attacked the army barracks in Buda, on Budaörsi Road. Several groups of freedom fighters and some Hungarian army units launched counterattacks. But resistance against such overwhelming force proved futile. It is estimated that more than 2,500 Hungarians and 720 Soviet soldiers were killed in the fighting.

Imre Nagy's call for help in the early hours of November 4 was heard worldwide. The United Nations immediately held numerous meetings and wrote several reports. On November 4, 1956, UN Security Council Resolution 120, considering "the grave situation created by the Union of Soviet Socialist Republics in the suppression of the Hungarian people in asserting their rights," was adopted with ten votes in favor and one, the Soviet Union's, against. An emergency special session of the General Assembly discussed the situation, but in the end, Secretary-General Dag Hammarsk-jöld and the UN did nothing. Krishna Menon, the represent-ative from India, always very critical of the United States, expressed sympathy with Soviet policies and voted against the UN resolution requesting the withdrawal of Soviet troops from Hungary. Three weeks later, after pressure from New Delhi, Menon reversed his vote.

While sporadic fighting continued for a few more days outside the city, the battle was essentially over. Other forms of resistance continued, however. The workers declared a general strike that lasted weeks. The steelworkers and coal miners held out the longest. Ironically, they were the very elements who were supposed to be the strongest pillars of Communism. By January 1957, a new Soviet-installed gov-ernment had suppressed all public opposition. Mass arrests, executions, and denunciations continued for months. According to the best estimates, the courts accused twen-ty-six thousand of crimes, sentenced twenty-two thousand, imprisoned thirteen thousand, and executed several hun-dred. Hundreds were deported to the Soviet Union.

The United Nations had promised anonymity to the hundreds of Hungarian refugees interviewed for its report. The Russians demanded the list of these names. Paul Bang-Jensen, the Danish diplomat in charge of the interrogation, refused to surrender the list. He was then investigated and hounded out of his position. Three years later, on Thanksgiv-ing Day 1959, Bang-Jensen was found dead on a bench in a New York park, gun in hand, a suicide note on his body.

Some of the revolution's leaders were captured and later executed. Others left Hungary or found sanctuary. Joseph Cardinal Mindszenty was granted political asylum at the United States embassy in Budapest, where he lived for the next fifteen years. He refused the authorities' offers allowing him to leave, insisting he would not go until the government reversed his 1949 conviction for treason. Eventually, in September 1971, in response to a request from the Vatican and because of his poor health, he left the embassy and went to Austria.

Imre Nagy found refuge at the Yugoslavian embassy. The Russians promised him safe conduct should he leave his sanctuary. He accepted the offer but was arrested minutes after leaving the embassy grounds. After a secret trial at which he was accused of high treason, Nagy was executed in June 1958, along with Pál Maléter, Miklós Gimes, and several others.

Most of the books that describe the causes and consequences of the 1956 Hungarian Revolution agree that the revolution was a spontaneous uprising. Only the Russians and some Western Communist parties claimed it was an action of capitalist-imperialist warmongers, Nazis, or some other reactionary element. Several historians have pointed out that our revolution was probably the only one with no looting. In fact, people suddenly became so unselfish and honest that baskets were set out at several street corners with the following sign on them: "If you can, donate money for those who have suffered losses during the fighting. If you have lost your home or valuables, take some money from here." The baskets were usually full of banknotes.

Some leftists completely misunderstood and purposely misinterpreted our aims by stating that all we wanted was a different form of Communism. But most of the analysts went deeper and came much closer to the truth: we wanted to be free and independent; we wanted a multiparty, democratic system; we wanted the Russian occupying troops to leave our country; and we did not want to continue to live under any type of Communism. We lost our fight, but our revolution shook the world. By exposing the horrors of Stalinist Russia and the Communist system, we managed to open many eyes in the complacent West.

The January 7, 1957, issue of *Time* magazine named the Hungarian Freedom Fighter the Man of the Year. In contrast, some American leftists could not—and still cannot—accept that the Communist economy did not work for the people—that it was sustained by an oppressive and tyrannical political system. I even had a boss at a US corporation where I later worked insist that Communism is good and necessary. He said that no one should believe us refugees, as we represent a minority opposition, evidenced by the fact that only 250,000 of us left, whereas 9.75 million people chose to remain in Hungary. Others have maintained that if the Communist system were as bad as we claimed, a third of the world would not have selected to live under its tenets.

By suppressing our revolution, the Soviets strengthened their control over Central Europe but alienated most Western Marxists. The events in Hungary produced ideological fractures within the Communist parties of Western Europe. For example, Italian Communist Party hard-liners followed Moscow's line, while the moderates were more sympathetic to the revolutionaries. Pietro Nenni, national secretary of the Italian Socialist Party, up to this time a close ally of the PCI (Communist Party of Italy), openly opposed the Soviet intervention.

In France, Nobel prize–winning author Albert Camus condemned the Soviet crushing of the Hungarian Revolution in a March 1957 essay published in *Franc-Tireur*. "The blood of the Hungarians," he wrote, "has risen too precious to Europe and to freedom for us not to be jealous of it to the last drop." Camus died in a 1960 car crash that was rumored to have been a KGB-engineered act of retribution for denouncing Soviet actions in Hungary.

During the uprising, the Hungarian-language programs of Radio Free Europe aired news of the political and military situation, as well as appeals to Hungarians to fight Soviet forces that included tactical advice on resistance methods. Later, Radio Free Europe was criticized for having misled the Hungarian people by promising NATO or United Nations intervention, an intervention that was never seriously considered.

The defeat of the revolution had long-term tragic consequences, with Hungary remaining under Soviet control for more than three decades. János Kádár became the head of state in 1956, a position he held until 1988. After a few years of executions, arrests, and other forms of vengeance, the Kádár regime created a less brutal, more open system that was commonly known as Gulyás (Goulash) Communism. Its intent was reflected in Kádár's official slogan: "Anyone not against us is with us."

Failed revolutions can become historically potent forces. The 1956 Hungarian Revolution was later hailed as the first nail in the Soviet empire's coffin. Although it took nearly thirty-five years, Hungary eventually became free again.

After the fall of Communism in 1989, on the thirty-third anniversary of the revolution, Hungary became a republic, instead of a people's republic. On June 16, 1989, the thirtieth anniversary of his execution, Imre Nagy's body was reburied in Budapest in an emotional ceremony. October 23, the day the uprising began, is now a national holiday in Hungary. The last occupying Soviet troops left the country on June 19, 1991, and in December 1991, Boris Yeltsin officially apologized for Soviet actions in Hungary in 1956. Yeltsin repeated this apology in 1992 in a speech before the Hungarian Parliament.

Flight

AFTER THE DEFEAT of our revolution, about a quarter of million Hungarians left the country, most of them by way of Austria. Budapest is about 125 miles (200 km) from the Austrian border, and at the time, Austria was the only neutral country bordering Hungary. When the Russians sealed the Austrian border and reestablished the Iron Curtain, Yugoslavia remained the only choice for escape. The Yugoslavs put refugees in guarded camps but released them months later, allowing them to leave for any Western country.

A large percentage of the refugees were college students, recent graduates, and middle-aged professionals. This enormous brain drain benefited the host countries but had long-lasting negative effects on Hungary's economy, educational system, health care, and scientific progress.

Gabi and I were among the first to try to flee to Austria. I asked Pali, Gabi's older brother, to come with us. Gyuri Szabó gave me a map and the name of a relative living near Eisenstadt (known as Kismarton in Hungarian), just across the Austrian border, in case we needed it. Gabi had neither boots nor walking shoes. We borrowed two pairs of boots from friends living nearby. She soon found out that neither pair fit her.

Late one morning, the three of us started out on foot. To avoid suspicion, we carried no luggage. We had decided to leave all of our possessions behind.

We crossed two checkpoints on our way out of Buda. At the first one, a Hungarian ÁVH soldier asked for our identification papers and destination. We told him that Gabi's home was destroyed in the fighting and we were escorting her to stay with relatives in a village a short distance outside of Budapest. He let her pass but told Pali and I that we could not leave Budapest. Russian soldiers manned a second checkpoint three to four hundred feet (90 to 120 m) away. The ÁVH soldier accepted our argument that the Russian soldiers could pose dangers to an unaccompanied young woman and allowed us to escort Gabi past the Russian sentry, but then we were to return. To add weight to his words, he pointed his submachine gun at us as we walked toward the Russian sentry. The Russian had a Hungarian interpreter. We told him that the other guy had allowed all three of us to proceed. He translated this and the Russian waved us through. But with the first guy pointing his firearm at us, we didn't dare make a move. We kept talking to the interpreter. He told us that he had stood there over twenty-four hours because his promised relief had not shown up, and he was now cold, tired, and hungry. We expressed our sympathy and left only when a truck stopped at the first checkpoint, concealing us from the eyes of the ÁVH man. We walked away as fast as we could.

After walking for an hour or two, Gabi developed blisters on her feet. She would not be able to walk much farther. Then a man came by on a rickety old bicycle. We bought his bicycle for a few hundred forints—this was a lot of money in 1956—and a wristwatch. At the next village, we found a truck and asked the driver for a lift. He said he could take us but not the bicycle. We left the bicycle on the road and climbed aboard, joining about two dozen others.

Late that afternoon, we stopped at another checkpoint, this one manned by a group of Hungarian soldiers fighting on our side. They had a tank. They were about halfway through checking our documents when a Russian tank appeared on the road behind us and stopped as soon as it saw the Hungarian tank. The Hungarian tank then pulled up on the road and pointed its gun at the Russian tank. The soldiers told us to go. Our driver drove away from this potential confrontation as fast as he could.

It was already dark when we arrived in Győr, one of Hungary's largest cities. Győr is seventy-five miles (121 km) from Budapest and more than halfway to the Austrian border. We soon found a bus on its way to the border to pick up blood and medicines from the International Red Cross. The passengers claimed they were going to handle the blood and other supplies.

The bus stopped at the border station, which was manned by Green ÁVH, border guards with a green band around their hats (rather than the blue bands of the regular ÁVH). The three of us slipped off the bus and hid in the shadows while one of the ÁVH men talked with the driver. A uniformed Austrian man approached us and said that he could see that we would like to go over to Austria. He told us to follow him around the gate, and if any of the ÁVH men should ask anything, we should just say, "Wir sind Österreicher" (We are Austrian). I followed him, Gabi right behind me, and Pali behind her. When Pali came to the gate, one of the ÁVH men asked him where he was going. Before Pali could answer, our benefactor proclaimed that we were all Austrians. The ÁVH man then politely raised the gate for Pali.

And so we crossed the Iron Curtain. It was midnight, it rained a little, and it was foggy. We knew that as long as we were in no man's land, the ÁVH could still recapture us, so we walked as fast as we could. When the lights of a car appeared behind us, we jumped into a roadside ditch full of mud. After the car passed, we continued walking, arriving at a small village an hour later. We entered the only house with its lights on, which was a tavern. Our Austrian benefactor was there. He asked, "Where were you? I came by with my car to give you a lift and save you from walking in this horrible weather." Everybody in the inn started laughing when we told him that when we saw the lights of his car, we jumped into the ditch. After we ate some hot food, he drove us to Eisenstadt, a few minutes away. By this time, it was past 2 a.m. The police station was the only place open, and the only quarters available were in the jail. The police apologized that regulations required them to lock all cell doors. Gabi was put in a cell with another refugee, a woman who had nightmares because of a bad experience crossing the border alone. And so we spent our first night in the Free World in a jail.

When we were let out the next morning, I asked the policeman if I could use his phone to call Gyuri Szabó's relative, Herr Patzenhofer. The police chief told us that Patzenhofer was one of the most important people in the area and made the call himself. He arrived within minutes, took us to a hotel, told us to stay there as long as we liked, and gave us some decent clothing. His daughter and daughter-in-law gave Gabi, who had worn men's clothing during the escape, some beautiful dresses. We have remained forever grateful for their help.

CHAPTER FIFTEEN

In the Free World (1956)

WALKING AROUND EISENSTADT, Gabi, Pali, and I found ourselves in a new and different world, with streets full of cars; shops with every type of meat, fruit, and other food; elegant clothing stores; and everything else the people of the West took for granted. We saw bananas and oranges for the first time in twelve years. And we saw our first jukebox.

I immediately established telephone contact with my parents in Cleveland. My father suggested that Gabi and I get married in a civil ceremony as soon as possible. This would ensure that we could immigrate to the United States as husband and wife. He also wired us some money. A few days later, we married in a civil ceremony at the former Esterházy Palace in Eisenstadt.

Two Italian newspaper reporters drove the three of us to Vienna. We had to go to the American consulate there to apply for immigration visas to the United States.

By this time, Vienna was full of Hungarian refugees, and we met several relatives and friends. Prince Esterházy invited two dozen recent refugees for daily lunches at his house. At first, we stayed at the Rathaus hotel near Vienna's City Hall. Then we went to stay at the house of a family in Grinzing, a lovely suburb of Vienna.

Both the Austrian government officials and the Austrian people were very helpful. One cashier did not accept our money at a movie theater; strangers invited us to their homes for lunch or dinner and offered us whatever we needed. One evening, as we were walking toward the train station to return to Grinzing, a car stopped and an elderly gentleman offered us a ride. On the way, he stopped at his home and returned with a large bottle of perfume for Gabi. He said that he knew that the Red Cross and other organizations were giving us clothes. But he also knew that a lady needs certain things beyond these essentials. It was touching.

We went to the American consulate every morning to inquire about immigration. During the afternoons, we went to see the Hofburg, Schönbrunn Palace, or Vienna's many museums and other attractions.

Pali decided to stay in Europe. He was admitted to the ETH (Swiss Federal Institute of Technology) in Zurich, one of the best universities on the continent. Four years later he graduated as an architect. He first worked in Switzerland, then moved to Bad Krozingen, near Freiburg, Germany. He lived in Germany until he passed away in the summer of 2009 at the age of seventy-nine.

One morning, as we stood in front of the consulate, an official came out and distributed little numbered pieces of paper to those waiting to enter. We got numbers 1 and 2. President Eisenhower had just ordered that five thousand refugees should get immigration visas to the United States without delay. We filled out forms, got chest X-rays to prove we did not have tuberculosis, and filled out more forms. We were to fly to New York on the first plane carrying refugees and were already sitting on a bus bound for the Schwechat airport when a consular official asked us and two young Catholic seminarians to follow him back to the consulate. Just as we were getting off the bus, a family of four, the Sterns, arrived from Innsbruck and took our seats. At the consulate, they told us that our X-rays had disappeared, so we could not leave on that plane.

The next day, we boarded a plane for Milwaukee that had been chartered by the Catholic Church and was operated by the Flying Tiger Line. We flew through a big storm and almost everyone on the plane got airsick. We were forced to land in Newfoundland until the storm passed and then continued our flight the next day. We arrived in Milwaukee on Friday, November 23, 1956.

In the United States

As I SPOKE some English, several newspaper reporters asked me questions about our revolution. Before we left Vienna, I had asked one of them to let my parents know that we were arriving in Milwaukee, so I was not surprised to see them waiting for us at the airport. But naturally, our family reunion had to wait until a television camera could record it, and one of the cameras had a problem. Ten minutes passed, then another ten minutes, and the policemen still kept us apart. Finally, my mother pushed a policeman out of her way and ran to us. After twelve long years, we could finally embrace each other. This was also the first time I met my youngest brother, György, who had been born in 1948 in Germany.

Our reunion after twelve years wasn't the only reason we became a media sensation. One other person and I were the only refugees on the plane with any knowledge of English. The reporters followed us everywhere, asking questions and taking pictures. Immigration processed us quickly, and by lunchtime, we had our Social Security cards. *Life* magazine arranged a lunch for us—a "wedding lunch" replete with a wedding cake. After lunch, one of the reporters, Dick Applegate, drove us to Chicago, where the Palmer House Hotel gave us a suite for the night. The next day, Dick showed us Chicago's most important attractions. We became good friends and invited him and his wife, Barbara, to our upcoming church wedding.

The following day, my brother Miki crammed the whole family into his car and drove from Chicago to Cleveland through a blinding blizzard. At one point, the car slid and spun 180 degrees, landing in the Indiana turnpike median strip facing traffic. There were six of us in that sedan, and we were very lucky no one was hurt.

A Wedding, a Media Blitz, and a New Job

MY FATHER AND Father Cassian Holbay, my former teacher at the Premonstratensian High School in Kassa, had already arranged our church wedding for December 1, just a week later, at the Hungarian Sacred Heart Church in Akron, Ohio. My brother Miki and Bertalan Fekete bácsi were the best men. It was a big event, with some seventy people in attendance. I knew only my immediate family and a couple of cousins, and Gabi knew only her aunt Erzsi, who had traveled to Ohio with her husband, Ludo, from their home in Toronto.

Reporters, some from Cleveland newspapers and others from the national media, continued calling me for interviews. They wanted stories about our revolution and asked for details of our personal adventures, how we liked America, and our plans. Most sent copies of the articles they wrote, and we filled a thick scrapbook with them and with photographs. A Cleveland television station invited me to appear on an evening talk show. The other guest that night was the world famous jazz musician and band leader Duke Ellington. There were also after-dinner lectures at meetings of various Hungarian associations, the Rotary Club, and other organizations.

Many of the news stories that appeared immediately on our landing in Milwaukee mentioned that I was a chemical engineer. As our arrival was broadcast nationwide, several companies offered me a job. One of these was a large mill and elevator company in Plainview, in the Texas Panhandle. The owner's secretary called me a few days after we arrived in Cleveland. The secretary was Hungarian and, as we later learned, was a good friend of Gabi's aunt Erzsi. He wanted me to fly to Plainview as soon as possible for an interview. When I told him that I couldn't go because of my wedding, he said that Gabi and I should fly after the wedding and spend our honeymoon there. The company sent us the tickets and some money for expenses.

And so, the day after our wedding, we left cold and soggy Cleveland behind us and arrived in warm and sunny Texas, stopping in Wichita, Kansas, along the way. The Wichita tarmac was covered with snow, and one of the stewardesses got off the plane to play in it. She later told me that she had never seen snow before, which surprised me.

We landed at the Amarillo airport and from there flew on the company owner's private plane to Plainview. The next day, I met Mr. Hill, the owner, who summarized his operation. Starch is added to plaster to slow down its hardening. Starch can be made from milo, and his company grew the milo (grain sorghum). His idea was to add milo directly to the plaster without first extracting and refining the starch. He needed an agricultural chemical engineer to work out the details. I immediately told him that I was an organic chemical engineer and that my previous experience was in pharmaceuticals and photochemistry. He agreed that the job was not for me but honored his offer to us to spend a holiday week in Plainview. He even arranged a trip for me to visit a university in Lubbock. We spent most of our free time with his Hungarian secretary and his wife. One evening, they took us to a drive-in movie theater, another first for us. The movie was about Billy the Kid.

Before we parted, Mr. Hill gave me some good advice about job hunting. He also made me promise to call him before I accepted a job because he wanted to be sure that I chose a good company.

A handful of job offers awaited me in Cleveland. I visited Ansco, a photographic company in Binghamton, New York. The Ansco job would have been interesting, and I could have used my training and experience. But I learned that before World War II, the company had been owned by a German conglomerate, was confiscated by the US government in 1941, and its future was uncertain. I was concerned about the company's future and therefore did not accept the job.

In January, I visited a few other companies and research institutes. Finally, after Mr. Hill assured me that Monsanto was a good choice, I accepted a job at its research laboratory in Dayton, Ohio. I started working there in February 1957.

The author and his wife, Gabi, arrive in Milwaukee, Wisconsin, November 23, 1956 (Photos of the arrival of the Hungarian refugees were taken by Randy McKay, Ernest Anheuser, Ray Hunholz, and Clarence Leino, all of the Milwaukee Sentinel staff)

From the Milwaukee Journal, *November 23, 1956 (Photos of the arrival of the Hungarian refugees were taken by Randy McKay, Ernest Anheuser, Ray Hunholz, and Clarence Leino, all of the* Milwaukee Sentinel *staff)*

Gabi, Miklós, and the author in Cleveland, Ohio, December 1956 (Photo by Zsigmond Csicsery)

The Csicsery family, reunited in Cleveland, Ohio, December 1956 (left to right): Pista Halász (a family friend), Gabi, the author, Pálma, Zsigmond, George, and Miklós and his wife, Maria, awaiting their first child. (Csicsery family archive)

*Gabi in Cleveland, January 22, 1957
(Photo by the author)*

*Gabi outside the family house on
Griffing Street in Cleveland in 1956
(Photo by the author)*

Akron, Ohio, church wedding, December 1, 1956 (Photographer unknown; courtesy of the author)

After the wedding in Akron, Ohio, December 1, 1956 (Courtesy of the author)

CHAPTER SIXTEEN

Dayton, Ohio (1957–59)

GABI AND I rented an apartment in a new development on Shroyer Road in Kettering, a southern suburb of Dayton. Every house in the development was a fourplex, with two upstairs apartments and two downstairs units. The only difference among the more than two hundred houses was that their exteriors were painted different colors. Some had stripes and one or two had large polka dots.

Most of our neighbors were young professionals. Four young men rented the apartment below ours, and we became good friends with them, especially with one, an engineer who worked for Yellow Pages. He greatly eased our transition into the suburban American lifestyle. He taught us how to prepare a steak and warned us not to fall for the many advertisements in our mailbox. One of the men played tuba in the Dayton Symphony Orchestra. He was extremely considerate, practicing primarily during the day when both of us were away from home.

Kettering was a very safe suburb. Some people left their doors open all the time so the milkman could put the milk in their refrigerator rather than leave it outside in the hot sun. Others left their doors unlocked even when they were on vacation for the neighborhood children who wanted to watch television. At that time, television was common but not ubiquitous. My parents, for example, never had a television while my father was alive, and my mother bought her first television in the early 1970s. During the 1950s, a whole family would go to dinner at a friend's house on a Sunday night and then watch a television program, like *The Ed Sullivan Show,* after the meal.

Various organizations in the Dayton area invited me to give after-dinner talks on the Hungarian Revolution, all of which were capped with a question-and-answer period. After my talk at a Rotary Club in a nearby town, one listener asked me whether the Soviets would start a new world war soon. I answered that they were in no shape for that at the present and would not be for at least another three years. The next day, the local newspaper's headline announced: "Hungarian Refugee Predicts World War III in Three Years." From then on, I accepted fewer speaking invitations.

During our first few months in Dayton, Gabi and I did not have a car and neither of us knew how to drive. I joined a ride group of four other Monsanto chemists who lived in the same development. One of them, Ed Mottus, was an Estonian Canadian chemist who was a few years older than the rest of us. He and his family became my and Gabi's best friends in Kettering. Eventually, Gabi and I bought a used 1951 Oldsmobile and both learned how to drive.

My first project at Monsanto's research laboratory was the development of a catalytic dehydrogenation process. John Andersen was my immediate boss, and Rudy Schuler was our manager. John taught me the operation of a continuous catalytic unit and also helped me overcome the difficulties of switching measurement systems, from the metric to the English system that was used in the United States.

Gabi found a job as a physical therapist's aide in a Dayton clinic run by a Dr. Bearzy. She primarily prepared bathtubs for patients with burns or with polio in what was a very hot, steamy environment. Dr. Bearzy's wife was Hungarian, and she kindly invited us to their home for dinner several times.

I remember how surprised we were when we saw that their teenage daughter's room was papered from the floor to the ceiling with photographs of Elvis Presley. Gabi soon learned to speak English, which helped her get a job she liked better at the public library in Dayton.

Back to School

GABI DECIDED TO enroll in evening classes in engineering drawing offered at the local YMCA. The first night she came home in tears. "I am the only woman in my class and all the men speak perfect English," she said, and then she pulled out of her bag a strange instrument that I had never seen before. It was a lettering guide that facilitated the writing of uniform characters in engineering drawings. Despite her rocky start, Gabi persevered and finished her first semester at the head of the class. This encouraged her to continue her studies at the University of Dayton, one of the ten largest Catholic colleges in the United States.

I attended evening classes, as well. The University of Cincinnati offered courses in Dayton, but when I applied for enrollment, I had no documents to prove that I had the necessary prerequisites. My adviser, Professor Jaffe, assured me that he had the same problem when he arrived in the United States from Nazi Germany, as he, too, had been unable to bring his diploma or any other papers with him. He told me to take one of the chemistry classes offered through the university's extension program, and if I did well, the university would accept my Hungarian degree. He also showed me a book published by, if I remember correctly, the University of Southern California that evaluated most of the world's universities. According to this book, eight years at a Hungarian gymnasium equaled an American high-school diploma plus two years of college. That would mean that my Hungarian diploma would amount to six years of university training, which would be equal to a master's of science degree from an American university. I enrolled in an organic chemistry class and received an A. I also passed the two language proficiency exams required for a PhD, German and Italian.

Professor Pierce W. Selwood of Northwestern University was one of several consultants at Monsanto's research laboratory. During one of his visits to our institute, I presented a status report on my research project. My talk impressed him and he advised me to get my doctorate. He suggested that I get in touch with Professor Herman Pines at Northwestern University, which I promptly did. After just one interview, Professor Pines accepted me as his graduate student. During my final months of employment at Monsanto, the company not only provided me with a fellowship but also allowed me to study for my university entrance exams during work hours. I remain grateful to Monsanto for all of its help during those days.

The New Environment

MOST OF THE many Hungarians living around Dayton had come from northeastern Hungary during the first decade of the twentieth century, and some of the older women had never learned to speak English. A much smaller number of the Hungarians had left after World War II. The balance, which amounted to just a handful, had escaped after the 1956 revolution. Gabi and I socialized mostly with this last group.

Once or twice each month, we drove to Cleveland to visit my parents. What I remember most about those journeys was that they took us through an Amish region. The Amish traveled in horse-drawn buggies—as they still do today—

because they did not believe in automobiles. Nor did they believe in putting a lamp on the rear of the buggies—"It is not in the Bible"—all of which were black. When it was dark, we had to drive very slowly to avoid collisions.

We found that summer in southern Ohio was very hot and extremely humid. Our apartment was on the second floor and poorly insulated, which meant the temperature frequently rose above 110°F (43°C), making our home uncomfortable even after sunset. Air-conditioned stores at the nearby Town & Country shopping center offered some relief, so we spent quite a few evenings in the supermarket or other stores. While wandering through the aisles of these shops, we familiarized ourselves with the wide variety of merchandise available.

We loved to swim, but there were no public swimming pools nearby, and the membership clubs were too expensive for us. During the previous decades, several small lakes had been created around Dayton by damming creeks. Because few people in Dayton knew how to swim, unlike in Cleveland and other communities on Lake Erie, only the shallowest areas in these manmade lakes, where swimming was nearly impossible, were open to the public. Lucky for us, one small lake was so new that the buoys to restrict swimming in deep water had not yet been installed, so that once we learned the lake's location, Gabi and I spent our summer weekends swimming there.

Swimming in deep water was so unusual in the Dayton area that more than once boaters, assuming that we were drowning, tried to save us. Another time, somebody contacted some reporters and sent them out to cover the story of people swimming in deep water. Every once in a while, we drove to Kentucky or Tennessee and spent the whole weekend there, as we could swim unhindered for as long as we liked.

On spring and fall weekends, we visited nearby state parks, several of which were established around prehistoric mounds. The largest such mound was in the city of Miamisburg, not far from Dayton. Most probably, people of the Adena culture built it between 1000 and 200 BC. The most interesting mound, which was probably less than a thousand years old, was known as Serpent Mound because it was shaped like a huge snake.

Other state parks in the area advertised what they called caves, though they were actually deep gorges that had been cut by rivers eons ago. Old Man's Cave and Ash Cave were the largest and most picturesque. Sometimes we met my parents and my brother György at these parks and spent the weekend together.

The National Museum of the United States Air Force, which is the world's largest aviation museum, is a short drive from Dayton. It housed hundreds of aircraft, and Gabi and I visited it often, sometimes with my parents and György and sometimes just the two of us. Most of the planes were US fighters and bombers used in World War II and the Korean War. The most interesting aircraft on display was a Soviet MiG-15, which a North Korean defector had flown to Seoul during the war. There were also many experimental aircraft, with the most unusual one a small egg-shaped fighter that was designed to be carried in the belly of a bomber. When an enemy plane attacked the bomber, it would release the little fighter to engage the attacker. After successfully shooting down the attacker, the little fighter would somehow return to the belly of the bomber. I think only this one prototype was ever built.

We also visited Cincinnati many times, where we would usually go to a museum or to open-air opera at the zoo. I remember Roberta Peters singing in competition with barking sea lions on one occasion. On another visit, we heard a concert by the Hungarian pianist György Cziffra, who, after spending years in a Communist prison, had left Hungary in 1956 and settled in France.

In 1957, we had only three days of vacation, so we knew we could not venture too far. We decided to drive to the Great Smoky Mountains National Park, where we slept in a little tent and ate what we could cook over a small propane gas burner. We saw wild bears and for the first time we met an American Indian. He had a beautiful war bonnet and sold gasoline to the tourists, who then photographed him.

The following year, we were entitled to a two-week vacation and set out in our car for Colorado. To save money, we put pillows and a mattress over the rear seat and slept in the car or, wherever it was possible, in our little tent. It was 100°F (38°C) in Denver, so after a day there, we drove up to Rocky Mountain National Park. These were the first real mountains we had ever seen. We hiked to see some lakes and waterfalls and climbed a small peak. We also drove to Pikes Peak, saw Garden of the Gods and the Red Rocks Amphitheatre near Colorado Springs, and toured the Leadville area. The high points of our vacation were views from Trail Ridge Road (highest point 12,183 feet [3,713 m]); the low point was the kitschy colored light show in a "musical" canyon.

CHAPTER SEVENTEEN

Northwestern University
(1959–61)

GABI AND I moved to Evanston, Illinois, a few months after I passed Northwestern University's four entrance examinations in inorganic, organic, physical, and analytical chemistry. We rented an apartment on Ridge Road, a short distance from the campus, and sold our Oldsmobile to save money. Gabi found a drafting job with A.C. Nielsen Company on Howard Street, which was the dividing line between Evanston and Chicago. Evanston was a dry city at that time, and all the businesses on the Chicago side of the street except A.C. Nielsen sold beer, wine, and whiskey. Once a week, Gabi cooked Hungarian *gulyás* for No Exit, a small café two blocks from the university. The clientele was mostly students, prices were low, and our earnings minuscule. After a few months, we discovered that the café did not refrigerate the *gulyás,* as Gabi had requested. Worried that it would spoil and make customers sick, Gabi stopped cooking for No Exit.

I worked at the Ipatieff Laboratory with Professor Herman Pines as my thesis advisor. Because I had passed all the entrance exams, I could start working on my thesis right away.

My objective was to elucidate the mechanism of *n*-octane aromatization over different chromia-alumina catalysts. I passed various branched C_8 paraffins over acidic and nonacidic chromia-alumina catalysts in a continuous flow reactor. Gas chromatographic analyses of the reaction products suggested eight- and seven-membered ring intermediates in the aromatization over the nonacidic catalyst. Aromatization involved five- or six-membered ring intermediates over the acidic catalyst. Experiments with ^{14}C-labeled n-octane confirmed these results. One of the most important petroleum-refining operations is the conversion of low-octane fractions to high-octane gasoline. My work contributed to the understanding of the role of catalyst acidity.

Away from Work

THE LABORATORY WAS in the basement of the Technical Building, which stood close to Lake Michigan. In the summer and early fall, Gabi came directly to the laboratory after finishing work and we would go to the lake for a long swim. Quite often, I also swam at lunchtime.

Lake Michigan cooled down in the fall and we could no longer swim, so we spent our weekends exploring the Loop, the heart of Chicago. We got to know the city's many excellent museums, with the Art Institute of Chicago and the Field Museum of Natural History our favorites. The latter is very big and we never did see all of its treasures. We also liked the Oriental Institute on the campus of the University of Chicago.

Most of our socializing was with other students working in the laboratory, with Hungarians enrolled at Northwestern, or with people we were introduced to through some mutual acquaintance. The students at the Ipatieff Laboratory were from all over the world—Italy, India, France, Japan, Israel, Poland, Taiwan, the United States. My best friends were Romano Covini from Milan and C. N. Pillai from Kerala.

We met Deneb Teleki, a Transylvanian Hungarian who became our best friend, at a movie theater. He overheard us discussing in Hungarian the beauty of certain parts of Sophia Loren's body. He has since moved to Albuquerque, and we visit him whenever we travel to New Mexico.

In July 1960, the Second International Congress on Catalysis was held in Paris, and Professor Pines suggested that I attend and that Gabi join me. At the conference, Professor Pines and Professor Selwood introduced me to several of the leading scientists in catalysis. Gyula Rabó and a handful of old friends and acquaintances from Hungary were there, too.

Gyula Rabó (1924–2016) was an assistant professor at the Technical University of Budapest when I studied there. After the 1956 Hungarian Revolution, he worked at Union Carbide and he is one of the principal inventors of zeolite catalysts. Our families had known each other since our grandparents' time.

During the conference, Gabi and I stayed at the Hôtel Saint-Louis en l'Isle on Île Saint- Louis in the center of Paris, a five-minute walk from the apse of Notre Dame Cathedral. The room, which cost two dollars a day, had a single bed that was narrow and U-shaped and a tiny washbasin. A spiral staircase led to all of the hotel's rooms, and next to the staircase was the one shower available to guests. At the beginning, we were concerned that it would always be occupied, but we soon discovered we were the only ones using it. After the conference, we stayed with Gabi's aunt Éva and her husband, Richard Pestalozzi, in Neuilly, near the Bois de Boulogne.

While we were in Paris, Gabi's brother Pali and my cousin András Tahy visited us for a few days. Pali and András were both attending ETH in Zürich and drove to Paris and back together. The four of us visited Versailles and Chartres and got caught up on what we had all been doing.

On our way to Paris we went to visit my dear friend Gyuri Szabó near London. Gyuri and Zsuzsa now had a little son, Andris. It was good to see them after four years. They took us to see as many of the sights of London as it was possible to get to in one week.

Our time in Paris at the conference, visiting the sights, and with friends and family was wonderful, but once we were back in Illinois, both Gabi and I were quick to get back to work. By spring 1961, I had completed most of the experimental work for my thesis, which meant it was time to start looking for a job. Chevron, 3M, Exxon, Mobil, Monsanto, Shell, UOP, and a few other companies invited me for interviews, and most of the jobs and the salaries offered were similar. I accepted Chevron's offer and was asked to report to the Richmond, California, office for work before the end of the year.

Then the hard part of my thesis work started. I was at the laboratory from early morning until late at night to complete the last few experiments. Instead of going home after work at A.C. Nielsen, Gabi came to the laboratory and helped me with the measurements. By mid-October, the experiments were completed and I submitted my thesis before the end of November. I passed my final examination and earned my doctorate in early December.[19]

We went shopping for a station wagon for making the move to California. We did not have enough money, however, so we had to buy it on credit. It was our first credit purchase, and it took a lot of negotiation because of our lack of a credit history.

A Cross-Country Road Trip

WE LEFT FOR California the morning after my final exam. With three weeks to get to our destination, we squeezed in a lot of sightseeing. The first night, we drove to Champaign to visit my friend Tamás Rédey, who was studying engineering at the Champaign-Urbana campus of the University of Illinois, and his wife, Emmy. Then, after spending a day each at Mammoth Cave National Park in Kentucky and in Memphis, Tennessee, we arrived in New Orleans. Our next stop was Houston, where we visited Professor Pines's daughter.

After stopping briefly in San Antonio to see the Alamo, we went to Big Bend National Park, where we saw real desert for the first time in our lives. We toured the park's two canyons and hiked in the hills. A trail guide we had picked up described the desert plants along the route. At one point, we saw some prickly pear cactus. According to the trail guide, the local Indians ate its fruits, but it did not mention that they first had to remove the spines. I picked one and bit into it. We spent the next half hour removing almost-invisible cactus spines from my tongue.

Following a hike on the white sands (composed of gypsum crystals) of New Mexico, we stopped briefly in Tombstone, Arizona. There we saw a reenactment of the famous Gunfight at the O.K. Corral. Two days later, we toured the Apache Trail. It was already dark when we found a campsite with a table. It was close to Christmas but surprisingly warm. We put the food we planned to eat on the table and went back to the car for plates and spoons. When we returned to the table, we found three ringtail cats munching on our meal. (Despite the name, the ringtail cat, or *Bassariscus astutus,* belongs to the raccoon family and lives in the arid regions of the southwestern United States and Mexico.) We chased the intruders off the table, but they continued to circle around us, ready to jump on the table whenever we let our guard down. It proved quite a sight, with the three lovely little animals running around the table and Gabi in nearly continuous pursuit.

Late Christmas Eve, we arrived at Grand Canyon Village, which stands at 6,860 feet (2,092 m). Because it was too cold to sleep in the station wagon, we checked the lodge, but it was full. The staff kindly found us a small room not usually rented to guests. The next morning, after the fog lifted, we enjoyed a fantastic view of the snow-covered canyon.

We saw the most gorgeous sunset as we approached Las Vegas. After a night there, we continued driving westward and spent a day hiking in Death Valley. It was late evening when we arrived in Bakersfield, California. Because the Central Valley was fogged in, we drove to Paso Robles and slept there. The next afternoon, I arrived at my new workplace in Richmond, California.

CHAPTER EIGHTEEN

California (1962–2017)

OUR FIRST RESIDENCE in California was at the Twin Oaks apartment complex on Sir Francis Drake Boulevard at what was then the northern edge of the Marin County town of Fairfax, about twenty miles (33 km) north of San Francisco. The complex included a large swimming pool that we used daily during the dry season.

Gabi and I worked five days a week and took two- and three-week vacations annually. We had season tickets to the San Francisco Opera and the San Francisco Symphony and later for Philharmonia Baroque Orchestra & Chorale concerts in Walnut Creek.

In 1964, we moved to an apartment in Greenbrae, much closer to both San Francisco and Richmond. Then, in late 1966, we bought a house in Lafayette, in Contra Costa County, twenty-five miles (40 km) east of San Francisco. The seller was Zoltán Stachó, who was moving to Boston. He had been a childhood friend of mine and his family had spent summers at Lake Balaton as I had. We moved into our new house soon after Christmas 1966 and still live there.

My Years at Chevron

MY EMPLOYER, CALIFORNIA Research Company, soon to be renamed Chevron Research Company, was the research arm of the Chevron Corporation, one of the seven petroleum companies that dominated the world oil industry in the early twentieth century.

Today, the Chevron Corporation is active in over 180 countries and is engaged in every aspect of the oil and gas industries, including exploration, production, refining and marketing, chemicals manufacturing, and sales. It has a long history going back to the Pacific Coast Oil Company, aka Coast Oil, founded in 1879. In 1900, the Standard Oil Company, a subsidiary of John D. Rockefeller's Standard Oil Company, acquired Coast Oil. In 1906, Coast Oil was reincorporated as Standard Oil Company (California). The company became independent in 1911 when the Sherman Antitrust Act broke up Standard Oil into its constituent parts. In 1926, there was another name change to Standard Oil Company of California, or SOCAL. "Chevron" came into use for some of the company's retail products during the 1930s. Eventually SOCAL changed its name to Chevron Corporation.

My first assignment was as a research chemist in the Exploratory Research Group. Later I moved to the Catalyst Research Group. My projects there covered several hetero-geneous catalyst systems used in various petroleum-refining processes and on the synthesis, characterization, and use of molecular sieves and shape selective catalysis. I developed several catalyst-testing procedures.[20]

My most important accomplishments included the discovery of restricted transition state type shape selectivity (the nonobvious type of three types of shape selective catalytic reactions) and the invention of dehydrocyclodimerization, the reaction converting C_3-C_5 paraffins to BTX (i.e. C_6-C_8) aromatics.

I also designed and supervised the construction of a multipoint catalyst + gas sampler device for the fluid catalytic cracker (FCC) catalyst regenerator unit. The results show how the catalyst circulates and how the coke is burned off in the regenerator. The results served to redesign the internal arrangements of the regenerator unit, and contributed to saving millions of dollars in FCC operation. The sampler was so successful that a second one was constructed for the FCC unit at another refinery.

I worked at Chevron Research for twenty-four years. In 1966, I was promoted to senior research chemist, and in 1970 to senior research associate. When Standard Oil of California and Gulf Oil merged in 1984, it was the largest merger in history at the time. Most of Gulf Oil's research personnel transferred to Chevron Research, adding to its size. In 1986, to shed excess personnel, Chevron offered early retirement to many of its employees close to the full retirement age of twenty-five years of service. I could not refuse this offer. However, I was too young to end my working life.

I had joined the American Chemical Society (ACS) in December 1956, and in the 1960s, after I began working at Chevron, I became a member the California Catalysis Society. I served as president of the society for a year, and then a few years later, I was named one of the directors of the North American Catalysis Society. I authored more than fifty publications, hold twenty-seven patents, and was frequently asked to be a plenary speaker at national and international conferences and a lecturer at research institutes.

Gabi's Years at AT&T

NOT LONG AFTER we arrived in California, Gabi was hired for a clerical position at an insurance company in San Francisco. The job required a long commute by bus from Fairfax, and it did not utilize her talents. Luckily, she soon found a job at Pacific Telephone and Telegraph Company that used her considerable training in drafting, and after some time there, she was promoted to manager of her group. Throughout the years, the company frequently changed its name to comply with various governmental antitrust regulations. In 1984, Pacific Telephone and Telegraph Company became Pacific Bell (PacBell), then Southwestern Bell Corporation (SBC), and finally AT&T.

In the 1980s, Gabi's department moved from San Francisco to Dublin, California, about forty miles (64 km) to the southeast of the city. Throughout all of the name and location changes, her group's work remained essentially the same: the design of circuit boards. One of the projects she worked on was the 911 emergency phone system. She also contributed to the development of a circuit board that helped blind baseball players hit incoming balls, a charity project of the company.

Gabi remained with AT&T for more than twenty-five years, retiring on December 31, 1987.

My Consulting Career

AFTER MY RETIREMENT from Chevron, I started consulting on various aspects of catalysis, in the synthesis, application, and marketing of molecular sieve catalysts, in environmental catalysis, in petroleum and petrochemical processing, and in other related areas. My clients included the Jet Propulsion Laboratory (JPL), SRI International, Catalytica Associates, The Catalyst Group, and other companies in the United States; EniChem and Eniricerche in Italy; Neste Oy in Finland; the United Nations Industrial Development Organization; and companies and government entities in India, China, and other Asian countries; Africa; Europe; and South America. As a United Nations chief technical advisor, I directed a five-year project on the application, development, and commercialization of zeolite catalysts at the National Chemical Laboratory of India. Years later I heard that the project was so successful that it received the UN's prestigious Centre of Excellence Award.

I enjoyed being a consultant, especially in Finland, India, and Italy. My projects were interesting and my coworkers were wonderful and talented. I became good friends with many of them, returning for visits years after the work was completed. In addition to consulting, I gave lectures at industrial research institutions and universities in almost every western European country and in Malaysia, Australia, New Zealand, Mexico, and South Africa. One year, I taught a short course on zeolite catalysis at the University of Szeged in southern Hungary. On December 1, 2001, I became a member of the Hungarian Academy of Sciences.

Throughout my consulting career, I tried to solve problems by encouraging cross-disciplinary research. In my area, cooperation between chemists, chemical engineers, and physicists frequently leads to great discoveries. International cooperation further enhances the positive results. On the Indian project, for example, I invited scientists from dozens of countries for two- or three-week visits, and sent Indian researchers to European and American institutes for longer periods.

I believe that this world benefits greatly when people familiarize themselves with the cultures and customs of other societies. Exposure to other cultures helps people recognize that ideas and practices are not necessarily bad just because they are unfamiliar.

I stopped my consulting work during the Recession of 2008. Most companies and other institutions cut their budgets for outside consultants during this sharp economic downturn.

Passings

IN THE FALL of 1962, my father suffered a heart attack, and he passed away on November 20, 1962, at the age of sixty-two. At first, he was buried in a Cleveland cemetery, but when my mother could not agree with the authorities at the Catholic cemetery in Cleveland about the non-Christian figures on the family crest she wanted on his headstone, she had him disinterred and cremated. The box with his ashes sat in her apartment until September 1973, when she traveled to Hungary and placed the ashes in the Tahy family crypt in Balatonszemes.

My mother stayed with us for a while after my father's death. We were hoping that she would move to California permanently, but she decided to continue her work at the Cleveland Art Museum, where she had gradually worked her way up to department director at the museum's slide library. Upon retiring, she continued to work privately for Sherman Lee, the museum's former director and a renowned authority on Asian art.

Around 1973, she moved to Ashtabula, a small coal port about seventy miles (117 km) northeast of Cleveland. A close friend from the museum slide department lived there with his mother, and my mother found herself at the beach whenever she visited them. The lake reminded her of Lake Balaton and her childhood, so she found an apartment only a few minutes' drive from the water's edge. She went to the beach daily during the twenty-seven years she lived in Ashtabula. She would spend an hour or two walking along Walnut Beach, and during the summer and fall, she was able to swim almost every day.

At age eighty-eight, at her children's urging, she stopped driving, and after a few minor strokes, at ninety-two, she moved to the San Francisco Bay Area to live at the Aegis assisted living residence in Moraga. Her new home was only ten minutes by car or thirty minutes by bicycle from our house in Lafayette. Gabi and I talked to her daily and visited her at least once a week. In early March of 2003, she fell in her room and fractured her hip. An operation could not save her. On March 29, 2003, she passed away in Danville, California. She was ninety-five years old. Her remains were cremated and, within a year of her death, her ashes were placed in the Tahy family crypt in Balatonszemes, next to my father's ashes.

In 1963, my brother Miki, who had lived in Cleveland since his arrival in America at the age of fourteen, was able to transfer within the General Electric Company from Cleveland to a lab in Sunol, California. He and his family moved to nearby Livermore, about thirty miles (48 km) from Lafayette. On December 3, 1978, Miki died unexpectedly of a heart attack and is buried in Livermore. His death deeply shocked all of us. I still miss him very much.

The author at Chevron, ca. 1966 (Photo courtesy of Chevron Research Company, Richmond, California)

The author in 1986 (Photo courtesy Chevron Research Company, Richmond, California)

WORKSHOP
CHALLENGES IN ZEOLITE SYNTHESIS AND CATALYSIS

KEYNOTE LECTURES
ROUND-TABLE DISCUSSIONS
SHORT COMMUNICATIONS
POSTER SESSION

A tribute to Sigmund Csicsery and Herman van Bekkum

Liblice Castle - July 10-13, 2010

INVITED SPEAKER
Avelino Corma

Organizers: Jiří Čejka - Kyung Byung Yoon - Joaquín Pérez Pariente
Under the Auspices of FEZA

Contact: zeolite2010@jh-inst.cas.cz

www.jh-inst.cas.cz/~zeolite2010

A workshop in tribute to the author and Herman van Bekkum, 2010 (Courtesy of the author)

VOLUME 53 (2010)
Nos. 19–20

ISSN 1022-5528
Published December 2010

TOPICS in CATALYSIS

Editors-in-Chief:
Norbert Kruse - Gabor A. Somorjai

CHALLENGES IN ZEOLITE SYNTHESIS AND CATALYSIS

A Tribute to Sigmund Csicsery and Herman van Bekkum

Editors:
Jiří Čejka
Kyung Byung Yoon
Joaquín Peréz-Pariente

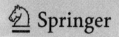

Available online
www.springerlink.com

Publication in tribute to the author and Herman van Bekkum, 2010 (Courtesy of Springer Verlag)

CHAPTER NINETEEN

Hiking, Climbing, and Traveling

THE MOUNTAINS, SEACOAST, lakes, and deserts of California offer unlimited opportunities to hike, swim, ski, or just enjoy beautiful scenery. At first, Gabi and I took only one-day hikes on weekend trips to Yosemite National Park and other trails in the Sierra Nevada and the coastal range. After we purchased Kelty backpacks with aluminum frames and goose-down sleeping bags, we began taking long backpacking trips.

In the summer of 1963, on our first long vacation in California, we hiked for two weeks in the High Sierra. Starting at Whitney Portal, we hiked to the top of Mount Whitney, then continued north across Forester Pass and Glenn Pass to Rae Lakes. On the way, we climbed Mount Barnard and spent a few days fishing for golden trout in the Wright Lakes and in Lake Reflection. We slept under the stars and were lucky it rained only once. After crossing Kearsarge Pass, which stands at 11,760 feet (3,584 m), we ended our hike at Onion Valley. It was an unforgettable experience, and we became addicted to backpacking.

The next summer, we took another long hike in the Sierra Nevada in the Minarets area. We made our way from Agnew Meadows to Thousand Island Lake, then along Garnet, Ediza, Iceberg, Cecile, and Minaret Lakes to Devil's Postpile National Monument.

The following year, we circled the Palisades in the central Sierra Nevada. The beauty of the Palisades equals that of the Minarets, but the Palisades are more rugged, the hikes are steeper, and the trails run 2,000 to 3,000 feet (600 to 900 m) higher than those in the Minarets region. We climbed Mount Sill, one of the highest peaks in the Palisades. On the penultimate day of our hike, we had to descend the snow-covered Southfork Pass. It was late afternoon and the sun was disappearing behind the mountains. As soon as the shade reached the slope, the soft snow froze. We slipped on the ice and tumbled down the steep slope. Fortunately, other than the fright, we suffered no injuries. But we decided that if we were going to continue hiking in the mountains, we not only had to buy a tent—we were still sleeping under the stars—but we had also better learn how to use ropes, ice axes, and other climbing gear.

A few months later, we enrolled in a Sierra Club rock climbing course. We practiced on Indian Rock and other small rock faces in Berkeley, eventually graduating to steeper granite walls in the Sierra Nevada. We also took lessons in snow mountaineering. Our instructors were volunteers, all of them excellent climbers and dedicated teachers, including some world-famous climbers. We are forever grateful for their efforts.

The rock climbing section of the Sierra Club (which no longer formally exists) organized climbing trips for almost every weekend, and once we learned the basics, we took part in several of them. On other weekends, Gabi and I climbed alone.

In addition to climbing, we took long hikes in the deserts of Southern California and Arizona. On the three-day Memorial Day weekend of 1965, we hiked down to the Colorado River and back inside the Grand Canyon. This was the first of our many Grand Canyon hikes. Sometimes we hiked from the South Rim, sometimes from the North Rim, sometimes on less-well-used trails into different sections of the canyon, and three times to Havasu Canyon. I consider Havasu Canyon to be one of the most beautiful parts of the United States. The long and arduous loop trail through Thunder River and Deer Creek was the most interesting of our Grand Canyon hikes.

In November 1967, we went to Mexico with a Sierra Club mountaineering group. We climbed three of Mexico's numerous volcanoes: Popocatépetl, Iztaccíhuatl, and La Malinche, at 17,802, 17,160, and 14,636 feet (5,426, 5,230, and 4,461 m), respectively. The next summer, with another Sierra Club group, we spent two weeks in British Columbia. We started by going up the Tchaikazan River Valley to Tchaikazan Glacier. As we approached the glacier, we passed a cairn that had been erected by a group in the early fifties to mark the toe of the glacier. In less than two decades, the glacier had retreated a few hundred yards. When we reached the toe of the glacier, we erected a large cairn to mark its current location. This was the first time we became aware of global warming.

The next day, we reached the head of the glacier, where we crossed over to the Lord Glacier. The uphill part of the divide was relatively easy, but it still took the better part of an afternoon to reach the top of the divide. The other side of this ridge was a vertical precipice. The only way to descend was by rappelling. Gabi and I were selected to belay down the other ten members of the group. The descent was very slow, as most of the others had never rappelled before. We had to explain to each person how to tie in, how to use their legs, and how to control their descent. Only half of the group was down when Tom, our leader, called up that we should not let anyone else descend because there was no place for them. It was already dark. Gabi, two others, and I had to sleep on the nearly vertical icy wall, hanging on two pitons each. Then it started to snow. We covered ourselves with the rainfly of our tent and tried to stay dry. It was a long and miserable night. At daybreak, we completed our descent. The others who had gone ahead were clustered at the bottom of the deep bergschrund that separated the rock wall from the glacier. As far as we knew, our group was the first ever to cross this divide.

Hiking back along the Lord River to civilization was an anticlimax. Unfortunately, one member of our group, a geologist, fractured her ankle. The assistant leader rushed ahead and returned the next day with a horse for the injured woman. On the way back to California, Gabi and I climbed Mount Rainier.

In the summer of 1969, we hiked in the Teton Range for a week, and then spent a week in the Wind River Range, where we climbed Mount Gannett. Two years later, in 1970, we hiked in the Swiss Alps and climbed Mönch mountain in the Bernese Oberland.

In 1973, we were invited by Gabi's aunt Éva and her husband, Richard Pestalozzi, who was Swiss ambassador to Kenya, to visit them in Nairobi. We received permission from our employers to add a few unpaid weeks to our regular vacations, which helped ensure the trip would be unforgettable. We climbed Mount Kilimanjaro (19,341 feet, 5,895 m) and Point Lenana, Mount Kenya's third highest peak at 16,354 feet (4,985 m); drove north to Lake Rudolf (renamed Lake Turkana in 1975) to watch a total solar eclipse; took a long safari through the Maasai Mara, Serengeti, Amboseli, Ngorongoro, Tsavo, and other national parks; and spent a week by the Indian Ocean in Malindi.

In 1980, we climbed Mount Fuji in Japan. Actually, we climbed it twice. It was so foggy on our first ascent that we couldn't even see each other, so the next day, we went up again. In addition to touring Tokyo, we also visited Kyoto, Nara, Hiroshima, Nagasaki, Fukuoka, Sapporo, and several other cities and hiked on the islands of Kyūshū and Hokkaidō.

Two years later, in 1975, we hiked for two weeks along the Inca Trail in Peru with a Mountain Travel group. Our walk circled the mountains of Salcantay in the Cordillera Vilcabamba and Ausangate in the Cordillera Vilcanota. Our long trek ended at Machu Picchu, where we had enough time to climb the steep and exposed trail to the top of Huayna Picchu, the cone-shaped peak towering about 1,180 feet (360 m) above the ruins. We spent an extra week visiting the mysterious Nazca Lines in the desert, the gold museum in Lima, and took a short detour to Bolivia to see Lake Titicaca and the ruins of the ancient city of Tiwanaku (Tiahuanaco). Ever since high school, when I first heard about and saw pictures of Tiwanaku's Gate of the Sun, I wanted to see it. One of my oldest dreams had come true.

The following December, we trekked with a Mountain Travel group in the Khumbu region of the Himalaya. To get there, we flew from Kathmandu to the Lukla Aiport, which has a very short and steep runway and has been called the most dangerous airport in the world. From there, we hiked to Namche Bazaar and then along the Khumbu Glacier to the Mount Everest base camp. Ama Dablam, the most beautiful mountain of the Eastern Himalaya, towered to our right. We hiked up to the peaks of Gokyo Ri, which rise to 15,575 feet (5,357 m) and Kala Patthar on the south ridge of Pumori, each offering fantastic views of Mount Everest, still more than 10,000 feet (3,000 m) above us.

During the following years, we climbed in the Sierra Nevada and the Cascades in California, in the mountains and canyons of Nevada, Colorado, Oregon, Washington, and Utah, and in British Columbia. We descended the Barranca del Cobre to the Urique River in the State of Chihuahua, Mexico; climbed in France and South Africa; and hiked up as close as possible to the active crater on Mount Etna in Sicily. I also spent several weeks climbing in the Dolomites in northeastern Italy, and ascended Cerro Chirripó, the highest peak in Costa Rica at 12,533 feet (3,820 m). After we joined Desert Survivors in 2000, Gabi and I climbed many other peaks in the deserts of California and Nevada (see Appendix 2 for a list of the major peaks we climbed between 1962 and 2011).

In addition to climbing, we took numerous long hiking and backpacking treks. Most memorable among them were the Milford Track in New Zealand; a walking safari in the Hluhluwe-Umfolozi Game Reserve in Zululand South Africa, famous for its large population of white rhinoceros; a week-long walk across Iceland; a hike along the Na Pali coast of Kauai; the Annapurna base camp trek; and backpacking in Escalante Canyon in Arizona and other desert canyon walks.

On one 1975 climbing trip to Kearsarge and Dragon Peaks with Dr. Dénes Balázs (1924–94), the founder of the Hungarian Geographical Museum (Magyar Földrajzi Muzéum), I photographed Dr. Balázs. My photo was used as the basis for a sculpture of Dr. Balázs by Béla Domonkos, which now stands in front of the Hungarian Geographical Museum in Érd, near Budapest.

We also bicycled, windsurfed, and learned to ski. We usually skied around Lake Tahoe in Heavenly Valley, Squaw Valley, or Alpine Meadows, though occasionally we ventured farther afield, including to Sun Valley, Idaho, and the Swiss and Italian Alps.

We learned sea kayaking, which enabled us to see many beautiful places. Once we kayaked with a small group through the Yasawa Islands of Fiji, camping on a different island each night. When the waves were high, kayaking in the open ocean was thrilling. (Two famous events happened in the Yasawas. In 1789, cannibals chased Captain Bligh and his men from the HMS *Bounty* through the archipelago, and in 1980, the film *Blue Lagoon* was made there, showing the young actress Brooke Shields in the nude.) We also kayaked in the Sea of Cortez in Mexico and along the coast of Costa Rica.

We mastered river rafting, too. Our longer river-rafting trips included the Salmon River in Idaho and shorter excursions in Costa Rica. And wherever we could, we snorkeled. I went scuba diving in Moorea in Polynesia and in the Red Sea, as well.

A Hunger for Travel

BOTH GABI AND I have always loved traveling, and during the rule of Communism, travel—even within Hungary—was restricted. Once we were free to go almost anywhere around the globe, we wanted to see as many places as possible.

While I worked at Chevron, we used our vacations either to take long backpacking trips in the western United States and Canada or to visit Europe, Polynesia, Mexico, and Central America. Later, my consulting assignments gave us opportunities to see places in Asia, South America, Australia, New Zealand, and South Africa. We toured Easter Island, the place farthest from any other land; Ecuador and the Galapagos Islands; Ürümqi, the city farthest from any ocean; the Dead Sea, the lowest point in the world; and climbed two-thirds of the way up Mount Everest, the highest point in the world. We went to the top of Taipei 101, the skyscraper that ranked as the world's tallest building from 2004 until 2010, when an even taller building was erected in Dubai. We toured the sights of India from Kashmir and Sikkim and Darjeeling in the north to Kanyakumari (also known as Cape Comorin), the southernmost point on the Indian mainland. We traveled along sections of the Silk Road in Hunza and in Xinjiang (Chinese Turkestan), where I understood some words of the Uighur language. We visited Tibet, Lanzhou, and Xi'an in central China and several cities on China's east coast, visited tribes in remote valleys in Yunnan Province, and cruised along the Three Gorges section of the Yangtze River. We took cruises on the Aegean Sea, along the coast of Chile, and in Alaska.

Most recently, we went from Amsterdam to Budapest on a Rhine-Main-Danube river cruise. We were supposed to return to California on July 6, 2015, after our Amsterdam to Budapest river tour. At the airport, standing in the check-in line, with other passengers jostling and pushing behind us, Gabi fell. She fractured her left tibia in three places. At Merényi Hospital, the nearest traumatology center, her leg was put in a cast from the hip to the ankle. Fortunately, the bones were well aligned and therefore she did not need surgery. Ten days later, we were able to fly back to California.

Archeology has long fascinated both of us, and wherever we could, we visited ancient cities and ruins. Some of the more interesting sites we saw were Athens, Delphi, and the islands of Crete, Rhodes, Santorini, and Delos in Greece; the Holy Land; and Ephesus, Halicarnassus, the marble cities and rock-cut tombs of Lycia, and the churches, monks' quarters, and underground cities of Cappadocia in Turkey. We also particularly enjoyed Teotihuacan, Tula, Chichen Itza, Uxmal, Tikal, Cuzco, and other sites built by the Mayas, Toltecs, Zapotecs, Aztecs, Incas, and other pre-Columbian civilizations; Angkor in Cambodia; the Great Wall and the terra-cotta soldiers in Xi'an in China; the Taj Mahal, the cave temples of Ajanta and Ellora, the lovely temples of Khajuraho, the ruins of Hampi, and countless other sites in India; the pre-Columbian mounds in Ohio; and the Moai, the monumental stone statues of Easter Island.

For a time, my contracting created hardship for Gabi, as I was working abroad three or four times a year for four to six weeks at a time. Fortunately, once she retired, she was able to join me on my assignments. In Milan, for example, where I worked for extended periods, we would frequently go to the Duomo, my favorite cathedral in Europe. I have an enduring admiration for this beautiful white marble building and its thousands of statues. We liked visiting the city's ancient basilicas and many museums, and occasionally we were able to get tickets to an opera at La Scala. Once my work was done, we would take long trips through Sicily, Sardinia, and other regions of Italy. The same held true during my assignments in Finland and Estonia.

As Gabi and I get older, we are less active. In 1994, I had a mild heart attack. The quintuple bypass operation that followed was successful, and after a few weeks, I was able to resume normal life. Following my doctors' advice, I continued bicycling, hiking, and mountaineering for many more years.

. . .

ALTHOUGH WE TRIED to bring back only one or two souvenirs from each trip, we sometimes exceeded that goal, and our home now overflows with our acquisitions. Gabi collected plates on nearly every trip, and we have them from Transylvania, Hungary, Portugal, the Netherlands, Denmark, Rhodes, Italy, Michoacán, India, China, and Japan. We have miniatures from Rajasthan, two large bronze statues of Indian goddesses, Tibetan and Nepali prayer wheels, Maasai and Turkana spears and jewelry, and Andean coca-leaf pouches and hand-woven hats. I have a few natural zeolites and other crystals I collected in the Sierra Nevada in California and on the Deccan Traps lava fields near Pune, India. We have dolls and masks from Japan and Africa, pewterware from Malaysia, beautiful shells of snails and clams from around the world, and more. I have also long collected stamps, specializing in those issued by countries other than Hungary showing Hungarian people and other Hungarian subjects. Everything we have brings back wonderful memories (see Appendix 3 for a list of countries we have visited).

Gabi on Mount Cheops, Glacier National Park, British Columbia, Canada,
August 23, 1966 (Photo by the author)

On top of Popocatépetl, Mexico, November 24, 1967 (Photo by the author)

On top of Popocatépetl, Mexico, with Ixtaccihuatl in the background, November 24, 1967 (Photo by the author)

Gabi climbing Mount Abbot, Sierra Nevada, California, August 9, 1975 (Photo by the author)

The author on top of Mount Hood, Oregon, with Mount St. Helens in the background, September 7, 1971 (Photo by Gabrielle Csicsery)

Gabi wearing Maasai jewelry, 1973 (Photo by the author)

Gabi on Dragon Peak, Sierra Nevada, California, October 5, 1975 (Photo by the author)

Matterhorn, Sawtooth Ridge, Sierra Nevada, July 19, 1975 (Photo by the author)

On top of Point Lenana, Mount Kenya, July 5, 1973 (Photo by the author)

Gabi at Mono Lake, California, August 16, 1981 (Photo by the author)

Gabi on top of Huayna Picchu above Machu Picchu, Peru, August 18, 1982 (Photo by the author)

Inca ruins, Tambomachay, Peru, August 1982 (Photo by the author)

On top of Gokyo Ri, Nepal, with Mount Everest in the background, December 11, 1983 (Photo by the author)

On Lembert Dome, Yosemite National Park, October 4, 1996 (Photo by the author)

Toward Annapurna, with Machapuchare, or Fishtail, in the background, October 1991 (Photo by the author)

Ajanta, India, January 22, 1999
(Photo by the author)

Rajasthan, India, January 31, 1999 (Photo by the author)

Angkor Tom, Cambodia, March 2006 (Photo by the author)

Sigmund Csicsery with Long Neck Karen girls, Ban Nai Soi, Thailand, March 11, 2006 (Photo by Gabrielle Csicsery)

At the tomb of Alexander Csoma de Kőrös, Darjeeling, India, November 10, 2006 (Photo by the author)

Ahu Tongariki, Easter Island, Chile, January 28, 2008 (Photo by the author)

November 2007 (Photo by George Csicsery)

Tomb of the Ming Emperors, China, May 3, 2011 (Photo by the author)

Mount Tamalpais, California, March 7, 2009 (Photo by the author)

A Magyar Tudományos Akadémia
köztestülete

tagjává fogadta

Csicsery Zsigmondot

a külhoni magyar tudományosság jeles képviselőjét.
Mint köztestületünk tagja,
gyarapítsa ezután is a magyar, s így az egyetemes tudomány
eredményeit,
tovább öregbítve ezáltal hazánk jó hírét
szerte a világon.

Budapest, 2001. december 1.

Glatz Ferenc
a Magyar Tudományos Akadémia
elnöke

Admission into the Hungarian Academy of Sciences, 2001 (Courtesy of the author)

Potala Palace, Lhasa, Tibet, May 8, 2011 (Photo by the author)

The author accepting the Árpád Award in Cleveland, Ohio, November 26, 2011 (Photo courtesy of the Hungarian Association)

Commemorative talk in Walnut Creek, California, on the sixtieth anniversary of the Hungarian Revolution of 1956 in October 2016 (Photo by George Csicsery)

CHAPTER TWENTY

Rediscovering Hungary

GABI AND I did not dare visit Hungary for more than two decades after we left in 1956. In the summer of 1970, we were able to meet Gabi's parents and her younger brother, Miklós, and my uncle and godfather, Gyula bácsi, and his wife, Ella néni in Lovran, Yugoslavia. This was the last time I saw Gyula bácsi, as he passed away just three years later.

In 1977, Gabi flew to Budapest to visit her widowed father. When she returned, she told me that she thought it would be safe for me to visit Hungary. In 1978, I got an invitation to the International Zeolite Conference, to be held in Szeged. I was concerned that more than two decades after the revolution, they still might arrest me, or worse. I asked the US State Department for an opinion. They advised me that I would be safe if the Hungarian government issued me a visa. I took this advice, applied for a visa, and received it.

My fear subsided as soon as I crossed the border. Every official I dealt with—the border police, the city police to whom I still had to report the addresses where I stayed, and others—was polite and cooperative. It was very different from the way officials had acted in the 1950s. I relaxed further when the conference organizers asked me to open the conference with a short talk, and then later, I was surprised to learn that a book on metal catalysis I had cowritten with Dr. Zoltán Paál, a Hungarian research scientist, was being translated into Russian.

This visit gave me an opportunity to visit Kassa (today Košice, Slovakia), the city where I had lived with my family from 1939 to 1943 (see chapter three). Crossing from Hungary to Czechoslovakia was an altogether different experience. The border police emptied my entire suitcase, took every piece of printed material to an office (to be copied, I guess), and searched the other seven passengers in the train compartment. They found nothing suspicious in my luggage, but they took a ten ruble note from one of the ladies in the compartment.

In Kassa, I invited my former classmates for a class reunion. About two dozen of them attended. It was good to see these old friends after thirty-five years. During the following days, one of them, Kornél Eschwig-Hajts, drove me to the village of Csicser (Čičarovce), where our family name originates (see chapter two). The parish priest there directed us to a shepherd in his nineties who remembered the location of our family's house, where my grandfather was born. The people living at the house still remembered my grandfather, who had revisited his birthplace four decades earlier. They even produced an old photograph taken at that time. They told me that the house, built several centuries earlier, had walls some eighty-seven centimeters (a little less than three feet) thick. Legend had it that long ago a secret tunnel, now caved in, extended from the building for about a mile outside the village.

Kornél took me and two of our former classmates, Öcsi Oelschläger and Feri Magyar, to Rozsnyó, Krasznahorka, Eperjes, Lőcse, Bártfa, and other cities in the Szepesség, and to Poprád. (Slovak names for these places are Rožňava, Hrad Krásna Hôrka, Prešov, Levoča, Bardejov, all in the Spiš region, and Poprad, respectively.) We took a cable car to one of the highest peaks in the Tátra Mountains. In Késmárk (Kežmarok), we visited the Reverend Benedek Áldorfay, one of our former teachers.

When I was leaving Czechoslovakia, the border guard already knew where I had been and that there had been a reunion with my classmates. I learned later that the police had interrogated Kornél and asked him why he had taken an American to Csicser, which was so close to the Soviet border.

Back in Budapest, I invited about two dozen of my closest relatives and friends to a dinner, and then I spent a few days in Balatonszemes. Swimming in Lake Balaton again after twenty-two years was a great feeling.

Following my arrival in the United States in 1956, I had frequent recurring nightmares: of interrogation by the ÁVH, of being back in prison, of descending into a coal mine. The dreams stopped after my first return to Hungary.

I've since visited Hungary often. While consulting in Italy and Finland, I was able to visit more than once a year. It was good to see my relatives and their children and grandchildren, my high school and college classmates, and other friends. Whenever I had enough time, I traveled around Hungary to cities and regions I had never seen before. Sometimes alone or sometimes with friends, I journeyed to Debrecen, Eger, Hortobágy National Park, Kalocsa, Kőszeg, Pannonhalma, Pécs, Sopron, Szeged, and Szombathely, among other places. I also visited regions that are today part of Romania, Slovakia, and Ukraine. In Slovakia, I spent time again in Kassa, revisited many of the places that I had toured with Kornél in 1978, and visited Pozsony (Bratislava) and the High Tátra Mountains. I went to Csicser more than once.

In Romania, I not only toured the Székelyföld and other Hungarian-speaking regions but also some of the Csángó villages on the eastern slopes of the Carpathian Mountains and the extraordinary centuries-old painted Greek Orthodox churches of Bukovina. In the Transcarpathian region of Ukraine, I visited Munkács (Mukachevo), the city where my father had grown up and where my paternal great-grandfather, Tivadar Lehoczky, had established his archeological museum. I visited his grave at the crypt of the city's parish church, and I stopped at Ungvár (Uzhgorod), where his collection today forms part of the city's museum. My great-grandfather's memory is kept alive by this museum and by streets named after him in every major Transcarpathian city.

Nearby in Homok, the village where my Tahy (maternal) grandfather was born, I visited the grave of my maternal great-grandfather, Ferenc Tahy, and met Tahy cousins who still live in his house. In Beregszász (Beregovo), a memorial plaque honors my mother's cousin, Ferenc Pásztor, a Roman Catholic parish priest who died in 1951 in one of Stalin's Siberian Gulag camps. The plaque reads: "For the memory of Ferenc Pásztor, victim of Terror." I also saw Verecke Pass, where the Hungarians crossed the Carpathian Mountains to occupy Hungary in AD 896.

I was fortunate to be in Budapest in 1991, when the country celebrated the departure of the last occupying Russian troops (the Budapesti Búcsú, or "Farewell to Budapest"). Witnessing the fall of Communism in Hungary was an unforgettable experience.

Most of the friends, relatives, and other people I met during these visits were sympathetic to those of us who had left in 1956 and became "rich Americans." Now and then, I encounter people who resent our higher standard of living, however. They do not understand how difficult it was for us to start a new life, how hard we had to study and work. They seem to believe that we do not work at all and money just falls into our laps. Some of these people who have never been to the United States and have never learned to speak English explained everything about the United States to me. They often accused me of being brainwashed but never asked what I thought.

Naïvely, I thought that because of my experience with the United Nations and in several countries on four continents, I could help Hungarian research laboratories and institutions. But I was wrong. Once, working through a high-level planning institution, I offered my services without charge to whichever institution would welcome my help. Nobody was interested at that time. Only much later was I asked to lecture at various laboratories and academic institutions.

After the fall of Communism, foreign travel for Hungarians was no longer restricted. Over the years, Gabi and I have invited many of our relatives and friends for summer vacations. Most of our guests were high school or college age and our primary aim has been to give them an opportunity to learn English, to experience the lifestyles in the United States, and to come to understand that even if something differs from what they know, it is not necessarily bad.

We have taken most of our guests to tour national parks and cities around California and the Southwest. These are places very different from anything they would see in Europe. In addition to showing off the natural beauty of the American West, we wanted our guests, who had spent most of their lives in cities, to see how beautiful it is to sleep under the stars, how refreshing it is to wash in a freezing creek, how easy it is to survive a hailstorm in the open. With some of our more active guests, we walked to the bottom of the Grand Canyon or hiked or climbed in the Sierra Nevada, the Panamints, Arc Dome in the Toyabe Range in central Nevada, Mount St. Helens in Washington, or other mountains.

I hope that most of our guests felt the same sense of freedom and appreciation that I have long experienced when presented with the great natural beauty and wonders of the outdoors.

. . .

IN 2016, THE sixtieth anniversary of the Hungarian Revolution of 1956 was celebrated at several venues in the San Francisco Bay Area. The organizers asked me to be the keynote speaker in the East Bay. I talked about my personal memories of the events, such as the toppling of the Stalin statue, the struggle over the radio station, the arrival of the Soviet tanks, and the massacres at Parliament Square.

In that same year, the Budapest-based Friends of Hungary published a book of the recollections of some of the people who took part in these events. The book, published in both English and Hungarian, contains my experiences.[21]

Postscript

It is difficult to say which of the places that I lived as a child had the greatest influence in determining who I am today. Although I spent much more time in Budapest, I still think of myself as coming from Kassa, where I lived from the age of ten to fourteen. Equally important was Balatonszemes, where I spent most of my summers. Szemes, as we call it, was where I learned to love nature, discovered the joy of swimming, and came to understand a sense of home. My best friends remain people I met in Kassa and Balatonszemes.

The year at military school had the effect of turning a spoiled kid into a somewhat disciplined adult—though not entirely. I was still young enough to view the experiences of fleeing from the Soviet army in subzero weather and witnessing the defeat and collapse of Germany in 1945 as adventures. At the same time, I saw and comprehended the horrors of war. The most important trait I and many of my schoolmates acquired was the art of survival even under the most adverse conditions.

The harshest circumstances I ever experienced were during the half year I spent as a prisoner of war while I was a cadet. Those months taught me that adversity brings out selfishness and malevolence but also goodness and the will to help others.

That hardship helped prepare me for the twelve years of Communism and Soviet rule that followed. My will to survive and my hope for a better future were tested during the many dark years.

The highlight of my life was the 1956 Hungarian Revolution. For a few days, all that had been denied and suppressed for so long was cast off, and I felt that the highest aspirations of my generation were within reach: freedom, independence from occupation, and the right to make our own choices.

But those dreams were quickly crushed in Hungary, so I sought them in my new home, the United States. Once I arrived in the Free World and was reunited with my family, I had to restart my life and establish a new career. Those were challenging, often lean times, and I could not have made it without the loving care and companionship of my wife, Gabi.

My work was rewarding, and I've enjoyed seeing the fruits of my contributions in chemistry. The decades I spent consulting were the best of my professional life. Those years also helped expand the opportunities for the pursuit of many of my favorite activities: hiking, mountaineering, spending weeks in the wilderness, and visiting faraway lands.

The Sixteen Points of October 23, 1956

IN OCTOBER 1956, Hungarian students compiled a list of sixteen points detailing their demands for political reforms in Hungary. The demands were a direct challenge to the ruling Communist Party leadership and their masters in the Soviet Union. On October 23, the students entered the city's main broadcasting station and asked that their demands be broadcast. When the ÁVH detained the students, the people outside the station called for their release. The state security police then fired on the unarmed crowd.

Here are the students' demands. (Several versions of the sixteen points exist, differing only in minor details.)

We Demand

1. Immediate withdrawal of all Soviet troops in accordance with the provisions of the peace treaty.
2. A secret election of all new officers for the lower, middle, and upper echelons of the Hungarian Workers' Party. The new officers shall convene a party congress as soon as possible to elect a new Central Committee.
3. A new government must be constituted under the direction of Imre Nagy. All criminal leaders of the Stalin-Rákosi era must be immediately dismissed.

4. Open trials for the criminal activities of Mihály Farkas and his accomplices. Mátyás Rákosi, the person most responsible for the crimes of the recent past as well as for our country's ruin, should be returned to Hungary for trial by the People's Tribunal.

5. Secret elections throughout the country to elect a new National Assembly, with all political parties participating. We demand recognition of the right of workers to strike.

6. Revision and reexamination of all Hungarian-Soviet and Hungarian-Yugoslav relations in the fields of politics, economics, and cultural affairs, on a basis of complete political and economic equality and of noninterference in the internal affairs of one by the other.

7. The complete reorganization of Hungary's economic life under the direction of specialists. The entire economic system must be reexamined in the light of conditions in the country and in the vital interest of the Hungarian people.

8. Disclosure of our foreign trade agreements and the exact total of the endless reparations payments. We insist on an accurate and transparent accounting of uranium deposits in our country, their exploitation, and the concessions to the Russians in this area. We also demand that Hungary have the right to sell its uranium freely at world market prices for hard currency.

9. The complete revision of standards applied to industry and an immediate and radical salary adjustment for workers and intellectuals. We demand a minimum living wage for workers.

10. The reorganization of the current system for delivering a fixed quota of agricultural produce and livestock to the state, the utilization of agricultural products in a rational manner, and support for individual farmers that is equal to that extended to those in collectives.

11. Reviews by independent tribunals of all political and economic trials and the release and rehabilitation of all innocents. We demand the immediate return of all prisoners of war and all civilians deported to the Soviet Union, including prisoners sentenced outside Hungary.

12. Freedom of opinion, speech, and of the press and radio, as well as the creation of a high-circulation daily newspaper for the MEFESZ Organization (Hungarian Federation of University and College Students' Associations). We demand the release of all existing cadre records and their subsequent destruction.

13. Erection of a monument commemorating the heroes of the Hungarian Revolution of 1848 in place of the now-destroyed statue of Stalin, the symbol of Stalinist tyranny and political oppression.

14. Replacement of emblems foreign to the Hungarian people with the Kossuth-Cimer (the old Hungarian coat of arms of Kossuth). We demand new uniforms conforming to national traditions for the Hungarian army. We demand the reestablishment of March 15 and October 6 as national holidays on which schools will be closed.

15. The university students, together with the workers and the peasants, jointly declare unanimously and with enthusiasm their solidarity with the workers and students of Warsaw in their efforts to regain the independence of Poland.

16. We object to the armed intervention of the ÁVH (the secret police).

Other lists of demands also emphasized the establishment of a new, temporary government, the end of martial law, Hungary's right to quit the Warsaw Pact, the removal of all Soviet troops from the country, punishment of those responsible for the massacres, the release of all detainees, the organization at the earliest opportunity of local branches of MEFESZ, and the convening of a Youth Parliament on Saturday, October 27, at which delegates would represent all the nation's youth.

Mountains Climbed
1962–2011

DATE		MOUNTAIN	CLASS	LOCATION	HEIGHT	
					Feet	Meters
1962	6.2	Lembert Dome	1	Yosemite NP	9,450	2,880
	6.16	Sierra Buttes		Northern Sierra Nevada	8,615	2,626
	8.4	Mount Dana	1	Yosemite NP	13,053	3,979
	9.30	Snow Mountain		Mendocino County, California	7,040	2,146
1963	3.3	Mount St. Helena		Napa Valley	4,344	1,324
	5.18	Black Butte		Coastal Mountains, California	7,448	2,270
	5.30 -6.1	Havasu Canyon		Arizona		
	7.14	Fairview Dome	3	Yosemite NP	9,731	2,966
	8.11	Mount Whitney	1	Southern Sierra Nevada	14, 495	4,418
	8.14	Mount Barnard	2	Southern Sierra Nevada	13,990	4,264
	9.7	Lassen Peak		Northern California	10,457	3,187
	10.5	Lembert Dome	1	Yosemite NP	9,450	2,880
1964	5.2	Cone Peak		Santa Lucia Mountains, California	5,155	1,571
	5.15	Glacier Point & Half Dome Saddle		Yosemite NP	8,400	2,560
	5.30 -31	Telescope Peak		Death Valley NP	11,049	3,368

DATE		MOUNTAIN	CLASS	LOCATION	HEIGHT	
					Feet	**Meters**
	7.20	Banner-Ritter Saddle from North		Minarets, Sierra Nevada	~12,000	~3,660
	7.25	Volcanic Ridge	2-3	Minarets, Sierra Nevada	11,501	3,505
	8.23	Lassen Peak		Northern California	10,457	3,187
	9.27	North Peak	1	Yosemite NP	12,242	3,721
1965	5.29 -30	Grand Canyon, from South Rim		Grand Canyon NP		
	8.6	Mount Sill	2-3	Palisades, Sierra Nevada	14,162	4,317
	8.21	Lembert Dome	1	Yosemite NP	9,450	2,880
	8.29	San Gorgonio Mountain		Southern California	11,502	3,506
1966	4.16	San Rafael Mountain		Coastal Southern California	6,593	2,100
	5.14	Kaiser Peak		South-Central Sierra Nevada	10,320	3,146
	7.2	Mount Starr	2	Central Sierra Nevada	12,870	3,923
	7.24	Mount Lamarck	1	Central Sierra Nevada	13,417	4,090
	7.26	Goddard Divide		Central Sierra Nevada	13,081	3,987
	7.27	Mount Fiske	1	Central Sierra Nevada	13,524	4,122
	8.6	Mount Hoffman	2	Yosemite NP	10,836	3,303
	8.23	Mount Cheops		Glacier NP, British Columbia	8,516	2,595
	9.25	Matterhorn Peak & Peak 11900	2-3	Sawtooth Range, Yosemite NP	12,264	3,738
	10.16	Mount Dana	1	Yosemite NP	13,053	3,979
1967	5.27 -29	Havasu Canyon		Arizona		

DATE		MOUNTAIN	CLASS	LOCATION	HEIGHT	
					Feet	Meters
	6.25	Leavitt Peak (near Kennedy Meadows)		Sierra Nevada	11,570	3,527
	7.22	Cockscomb	4	Yosemite NP	11,040	3,365
	7.23	Echo Peaks	3-4	Yosemite NP	11,000	3,353
	8.5-6	Mount Dana, via Dana Glacier	3	Yosemite NP	13,053	3,979
	8.20	Mount Dade	2	Central Sierra Nevada	13,600	4,145
	9.23	Pyramid Peak		Desolation Wilderness, Sierra Nevada	9,983	3,043
	10.15	Sierra Buttes		Northern Sierra Nevada	8,615	2,626
	11.19	La Malinche (Matlalcueyetl)		Mexico	14,636	4,461
	11.22	Iztaccihuatl		Mexico	17,160	5,230
	11.24	Popocatépetl		Mexico	17,802	5,426
1968	5.4	Indian Rock-North Dome-Yosemite Point		Yosemite NP	8,522	2,598
	6.22 -23	Glacier, Black Rock, and Sawtooth Passes		Mineral King, Southern Sierra Nevada	11,200 -11,700	3,414 -3,566
	7.14	Mount Humphreys	4	Central Sierra Nevada	13,986	4,263
	7.28	Red Slate Mountain, via McGee Creek	1-2	Central Sierra Nevada	13,163	4,012
	8.16	Mount Friendly (fourth ascent!)		British Columbia Coast Range	8,800	2,682
	8.30	Mount Rainier		Washington	14,410	4,392
	11.9	Wildrose Peak		Death Valley NP	9,064	2,763
	11.9 -10	Telescope Peak		Panamint Range, Death Valley NP	11,049	3,368

DATE		MOUNTAIN	CLASS	LOCATION	HEIGHT	
					Feet	Meters
1969	5.11	Monolith-Three Sisters-Machette Ridge	4-5.5	Pinnacles National Monument, California		
	5.17	Sunnyside Bench	5	Yosemite NP		
	5.29 -31	Escalante River via Coyote Gulch		Southern Utah		
	6.15	Mount Tallac (near Lake Tahoe)		Northern Sierra Nevada	9,735	2,967
	7.5	White Mountain Peak		White Mountains, California	14,242	4,341
	7.26	Snow Mountain		Mendocino County, California	7,040	2,146
	8.4	Mount Woodring	2	Grand Teton NP	11,585	3,531
	8.7	South Teton	3	Grand Teton NP	12,505	3,812
	8.8	Static Peak	1	Grand Teton NP	11,294	3,442
	8.13	Gannett Peak	4	Wind River Range, Wyoming	13,785	4,202
	9.28	Red Slate Mountain, via Convict Lake	1-2	Central Sierra Nevada	13,163	4,012
1970	5.29 -30	Grand Canyon, from South Rim		Grand Canyon NP		
	7.5	Mount Agassiz	2	Palisades, Sierra Nevada	13,891	4,234
	7.12	Mount Shasta, South Face		Northern California	14,162	4,317
	8.2	Mount Ritter	3	Minarets, Central Sierra Nevada	13,157	4,010
	9.2	Mönch		Switzerland	13,448	4,099
1971	5.8	El Capitan		Yosemite NP	7,569	2,307
	5.9	Eagle Peak		Yosemite NP	7,779	2,371
	5.28 -29	Grand Canyon, from North Rim		Grand Canyon NP		
	5.31	Sunset Crater		Arizona		
	7.18	Mount Conness	2-3	Yosemite NP	12,590	3,837
	8.15	Mount Lyell	2-3	Yosemite NP	13,114	3,997

DATE		MOUNTAIN	CLASS	LOCATION	HEIGHT	
					Feet	Meters
	8.30	Mount Baker (impending storm turned us back below the summit)		Washington	(10,778)	(3,285)
	9.5	Matterhorn and Sacajawea Peaks		Wallowa Mountains, Eastern Oregon	9,832 -9,839	2,997 -2,999
	9.7	Mount Hood		Oregon	11,245	3,424
	9.25	Mount Morgan	1	Central Sierra Nevada	13,748	4,190
1972	4.15	Telescope Peak		Panamint Range, Death Valley NP	11,049	3,368
	8.5	Mount Agassiz	2	Palisades, Sierra Nevada	13,891	4,234
	9.3	Mount Tyndall	3	Southern Sierra Nevada	14,018	4,273
	9.23	Vogelsang Peak	1	Yosemite NP	11,516	3,510
	9.23	Fletcher Peak	2	Yosemite NP	11,408	3,477
	9.30	Mount Dana	1	Yosemite NP	13,053	3,979
	10.21	Half Dome		Yosemite NP	8,842	2,650
	11.25	Pinkley Peak		Organ Pipe Cactus NP	3,145	959
1973	6.13 -17	Mount Kilimanjaro (Kibo)		Tanzania	19,341	5,895
	7.3-6	Point Lenana – Mount Kenya		Kenya	16,355	4,985
	7.29	Boundary Peak		California/Nevada Border	13,140	4,005
	8.19	Middle Palisade	4	Palisades, Sierra Nevada	14,040	4,279
	9.2	Warren Peak		Warner Mountains, Northern California	9,710	2,960
	9.2	Eagle Peak		Warner Mountains, Northern California	9,892	3,015

DATE		MOUNTAIN	CLASS	LOCATION	HEIGHT	
					Feet	**Meters**
1974	5.26	Mount Shasta, North Face, via Bolam Glacier		Northern California	14,162	4,317
	7.5	Mount Ritter	3	Minarets, Central Sierra Nevada	13,157	4,010
	8.28	Glacier Peak		North Cascades, Washington	10,541	3,213
	11.28	Telescope Peak		Panamints, Death Valley NP	11,049	3,368
1975	5.23 -25	Grand Canyon, from North Rim, to Clear Creek		Grand Canyon NP		
	7.4	Olancha Peak		Southern Sierra Nevada	12,123	3,695
	7.19	Matterhorn Peak	2-3	Sawtooth Ridge, Yosemite NP	12,264	3,738
	8.9	Mount Abbot	3	Central Sierra Nevada	13,715	4,180
	8.31	North Palisade	3-4	Palisades, Sierra Nevada	14,242	4,341
	10.4	Kearsarge Peak	1	Southern Sierra Nevada	12,598	3,840
	10.5	Dragon Peak	3	Southern Sierra Nevada	12,955	3,949
	12.22	Volcano San Pedro		Lake Atitlan, Guatemala	9,918	3,023
	12.25	Volcano de Agua		Guatemala	12,310	3,752
1976	5.30	Mount Winchell	4	Palisades, Sierra Nevada	13,768	4,196
	6.20	Mount Clark (author dislocates shoulder)	3	Yosemite NP	11,522	3,512
	9.30	Uncompahgre Peak		Colorado	14,307	4,361
	10.1	Peak 13,106		Colorado	13,106	3,995
	11.25	Mount Dana	1	Yosemite NP	13,053	3,979

DATE		MOUNTAIN	CLASS	LOCATION	HEIGHT	
					Feet	Meters
1977	2.20	Peak 6491, Cottonwood Mountains		Death Valley NP	6,491	1,978
	7.3	Bear Creek Spire	3	Central Sierra Nevada	13,713	4,180
	7.17	Red Slate Mountain, via McGee Creek	1-2	Central Sierra Nevada	13,163	4,012
	8.17	Mount Olympus, West Peak		Washington (author falls into crevasse)	7,965	2,428
	9.4	Rodgers Peak	3	Central Sierra Nevada	12,978	3,956
1978	2.19	Peak 5198 (near Queen Mountain)		Joshua Tree NP	5198	1,584
	5.28	Thompson Ridge, near Baboon Lake		Central Sierra Nevada	~12,800	~3,900
	7.29	Mount Agassiz	2	Palisades, Sierra Nevada	13,891	4,234
	8.5	Sawtooth Ridge		Trinity Alps, Northern California	~ 7,500	~ 2,280
	8.6	Caribou Mountain		Trinity Alps, Northern California	8,575	2,615
	10.1	Volcanic Ridge, West Peak	2-3	Minarets, Sierra Nevada	~11,490	~3,502
	10.21	Pyramid Peak, from Twin Bridges		Desolation Valley, near Lake Tahoe, California	9,983	3,043
1979	6.24	Mount Shasta		Northern California	14,162	4,317
	7.7	Mount Conness	2-3	Yosemite NP	12,590	3,837
	7.8	Fairview Dome	3	Yosemite NP	9,731	2,966
	7.25	Reward Peak		Sawtooth Range, Idaho	10,074	3,071
	7.26	Elk Peak (100 feet below peak)		Sawtooth Range, Idaho	10,582	3,225

DATE		MOUNTAIN	CLASS	LOCATION	HEIGHT	
					Feet	**Meters**
	9.2	Tower Peak, and North Buttress		Yosemite NP	11,755	3,583
	9.6	American Fork		Wasatch Mountains, Utah	11,489	3,502
	9.6	Twin Peaks		Wasatch Mountains, Utah	11,433	3,485
1980	3.23	Mount Rogers		Panamints, Death Valley NP	9,994	3,046
	3.23	Mount Bennett		Panamints, Death Valley NP	9,980	3,042
	5.23 -25	From Grandview Pt. to Hance Rapid, and then to Cottonwood Camp		Grand Canyon NP		
	7.5	Fujiyama		Honshu, Japan	12,388	3,776
	7.6	Fujiyama		Honshu, Japan	12,388	3,776
	7.22	O-Akan		Hokkaido, Japan	4,498	1,371
	8.31	Striped Mountain and Peak 12905	2	Near Taboose Pass, Sierra Nevada	13,120+	4,000+
1981	6.28	Mount Ritter	3	Minarets, Central Sierra Nevada	13,157	4,010
	7.4	Volcanic Ridge	2-3	Minarets, Central Sierra Nevada	11,501	3,505
	7.26	Snowyside Mountain		Sawtooth Range, Idaho	10,651	3,247
	7.29	Squaretop Mountain	2-3	Wind River Range, Wyoming	11,695	3,565
	8.1	Fremont Peak	3	Wind River Range, Wyoming	13,745	4,189
	8.3	Stroud Peak	2	Wind River Range, Wyoming	12,198	3,718
	8.6	Mitchell Peak	2	Wind River Range, Wyoming	12,482	3,805
	8.15	Mount Agassiz	2	Palisades, Sierra Nevada	13,891	4,234

DATE		MOUNTAIN	CLASS	LOCATION	HEIGHT	
					Feet	Meters
	9.6	Split Mountain	2	Central Sierra Nevada	14,058	4,285
1982	5.29 -6.1	Thunder River, Deer Creek		Grand Canyon NP		
	7.18	Matterhorn Peak	2-3	Sawtooth Ridge, Yosemite NP	12,264	3,738
	8.23	Cerro Puca Punta		Cordillera Vilcanota, Peru	17,066	5,202
	10.9	Pyramid Peak, from Twin Bridges		Desolation Valley, near Lake Tahoe	9,983	3,043
	11.26	Whale Peak		Anza-Borrego Desert State Park	5,349	1,630
1983	2.19	Thimble Peak		Grapevine Mountains, Death Valley NP	6,381	1,945
	7.3	Mount Lyell	2-3	Yosemite NP	13,114	3,997
	7.31	Mount Baldwin	2	Near Convict Lake, Sierra Nevada	12,614	3,845
	9.3	Mount Agassiz	2	Palisades, Sierra Nevada	13,891	4,234
	12.7	Kala Pattar		Khumbu Region, Himalaya, Nepal	18,514	5,643
	12.8	Mount Everest Base Camp		Khumbu Glacier, Himalaya, Nepal	17,552	5,350
	12.9	Chola-La Pass		Himalaya, Nepal	17,782	5,420
	12.11	Gokyo- Ri		Himalaya, Nepal	17,575	5,357
1984	7.13	Seeblaskogel		Stubai Alps, Austria	10,613	3,235
	7.18	Ritterhorn		Dolomiti, Alto Adige, Italy	7,415	2,260
	7.20	Petz Schern/ Monte Sciliar		Dolomiti, Alto Adige, Italy	8412	2,564
	7.28	Mount Dade	2	Central Sierra Nevada	13,600	4,145
	8.11	Volcanic Ridge	2-3	Minarets, Sierra Nevada	11,501	3,505

DATE		MOUNTAIN	CLASS	LOCATION	HEIGHT	
					Feet	Meters
	8.19	Cleaver Peak	3	Sawtooth Ridge, Yosemite NP	11,760	3,584
	9.1	North Dragon Pass		Southern Sierra Nevada	12,400+	3,780+
	11.22	Mount San Jacinto		Southern California	10,804	3,293
	12.10	Barranca del Cobre, Rio Urique		Chihuahua, Mexico		
1985	6.9	Mount Shasta		Northern California	14,162	4,317
	7.7	Mount Davis	1	Yosemite NP	12,311	3,752
	8.3	Mount Agassiz	2	Palisades, Sierra Nevada	13,891	4,234
	9.1	Center Peak	1-2	Southern Sierra Nevada	12,760	3,889
	12.13	Chirripó Grande		Costa Rica	12,530	3,819
1986	7.16	Paternkofel/ Monte Paterno		Dolomiti di Sesto, Alto Adige, Italy	9,003	2,744
	7.17	Hochbrunner- schneide/Monte Popera		Dolomiti di Sesto, Alto Adige, Italy	9,993	3,046
1987	6.28	Mount Lamarck	1	Central Sierra Nevada	13,417	4,090
	7.9	Mount Dana	1	Yosemite NP	13,053	3,979
	8.1	Mount Agassiz	2	Palisades, Sierra Nevada	13,891	4,234
	9.11	Cima Tosa		Dolomiti di Brenta, Alto Adige, Italy	10,410	3,173
1988	6.21	Sahale Arm		North Cascades, Washington	6,800	2,073
	6.25	Avalanche Crest, Selkirks		Glacier NP, British Columbia	7,792	2,375
	7.4	Highest Pt. north of Mount Opal		Queen Elizabeth Ranges, Jasper NP	9,071	2,765
	7.5	Morro Peak		Jasper NP, Canada	5,500	1,676

DATE		MOUNTAIN	CLASS	LOCATION	HEIGHT	
					Feet	Meters
	7.8	Titkana Peak		Mount Robson PP, Canada	9,286	2,830
	7.12	Mount Oberlin	1-2	Glacier NP, Montana	8,100	2,469
	7.19	Hayden Peak		Uinta Mountains, Utah	12,480	3,804
1989	6.11	Carevolo		Apennines, Italy	~5,250	~1,600
	8.19	Two Teats	2-3	Central Sierra Nevada	11,387	3,471
	8.19	San Joaquin Mountain	1	Central Sierra Nevada	11,600	3,536
	8.20	Carson Peak	1	Central Sierra Nevada	10,909	3,325
	8.21	Mount Davis	1	Yosemite NP	12,311	3,752
	10.12	Table Mountain		Cape Province, South Africa	3,563	1,086
1990	8.5	Peak 7642		Trinity Alps, Northern California	7,642	2,329
1991	3.9-12	Milford Track; Mackinnon Pass		New Zealand, South Island	3,786	1,154
	9.14	Volcanic Ridge	2-3	Minarets, Sierra Nevada	11,501	3,505
	9.18	Bright Angel Trail, down and up in one day		Grand Canyon NP		
	10.26 -11.17	Annapurna South, Base Camp		Himalaya, Nepal	~13,700	~4,200
1992	8.28	Center Peak	1-2	Southern Sierra Nevada	12,760	3,889
	9.26	Sass Rigais		Dolomiti, Alto Adige, Italy	9,925	3,025
	9.27	Pizzes da Cir / Tschirspitzen		Dolomiti, Alto Adige, Italy	8,268	2,520
	11.9	Telescope Peak		Panamints, Death Valley NP	11,049	3,368
	11.12	Corkscrew Peak		Death Valley NP	5,804	1,769

DATE		MOUNTAIN	CLASS	LOCATION	HEIGHT	
					Feet	**Meters**
1993	4.24	Angel's Landing		Zion NP	5,990	1,825
	4.25	Observation Point		Zion NP		
	5.7	Plateau Point		Grand Canyon NP		
	7.25	Dick's Peak		Desolation Wilderness, Northern California	9,974	3,040
	8.26	Mount Brewer, South Summit Ridge	1	Kings Canyon NP	~13,450	~4,100
	10.24	Table Mountain via Plattenclipp		Cape Province, South Africa	3,563	1,086
	10.31	Perdekop, Franschhoek Mountains		Cape Province, South Africa	5,167	1,575
	12.3.	Wildrose Peak		Panamints, Death Valley NP	9,064	2,763
1994	6.21	Pic d'Aurelle, Le Trayas		Esterel Mountains, Provence, France	1,056	322
	6.21	Pic de Ours		Esterel Mountains, Provence, France	1,614	492
	6.21	Pic de Cap Roux		Esterel Mountains, Provence, France	1,486	453
1995	2.19	Carson Falls, Pine Mountain		Marin County, California		
	8.21	Shuksan Arm		North Cascades, Washington	5,538	1,688
	8.23	Sahale Arm		North Cascades, Washington	7,700	2,347
	8.29	Second Burroughs Mountain		Mount Rainier, Washington		
	8.30	Mount Margaret		Mount St. Helens Volcanic NP	8,585	2,617
1996	9.7	Matterhorn		Drakensberg, South Africa	6,545	1,995
	10.4	Lembert Dome	1	Yosemite NP	9,450	2,880

DATE		MOUNTAIN	CLASS	LOCATION	HEIGHT	
					Feet	Meters
	12.11	Turtlehead Peak		Red Rock Canyon, Nevada	6,323	1,927
1997	5.11	Cuyamaca Peak		Southern California	6,512	1,985
	5.12	Mount San Jacinto		Southern California	10,804	3,293
1998	5.4	Mount Etna (as far as volcanic activity allows)		Sicily, Italy	~9,840	~3,000
	7.25	Sierra Buttes		Northern Sierra, Nevada	8,615	2,626
	10.15	Mount Dana	1	Yosemite NP	13,053	3,979
1999	4.15	Peak 4769, and Pine Canyon		Joshua Tree NP	4,769	1,454
	7.11	Cone Peak		Coastal (Santa Lucia) Mountains	5,155	1,571
	8.2	Lembert Dome	1	Yosemite NP	9,450	2,880
	8.2	Mount Dana	1	Yosemite NP	13,053	3,979
	8.9 -10	Grand Canyon, from South Rim		Grand Canyon NP		
	9.29	Lassen Peak		Northern California	10,457	3,187
	9.30	Mount Scott		Crater Lake NP, Oregon	8,929	2,721
	10.2	South Sister		Cascades, Central Oregon	10,358	3,157
	10.5	Summit of Smith Rock		Smith Rock State Park, Oregon	3,300	1,006
	11.18	Mount San Jacinto		Southern California	10,804	3,293
2000	4.27	Table Top Mountain		Mojave National Reserve, California	6,176	1,882
	6.20	Punte Balestrieri, Monte Limbara		Gallura, Sardinia, Italy	4,459	1,359
	9.28	Reveille Range		Nevada	8,101	2,469
	10.1	Wheeler Peak		Eastern Nevada	13,063	3,982

DATE		MOUNTAIN	CLASS	LOCATION	HEIGHT	
					Feet	Meters
2001	7.22	Mount Hoffman	2	Yosemite NP	10,850	3,307
	7.23	Bishop Pass		Kings Canyon NP	11,972	3,649
	8.7	Lassen Peak		Northern California	10,457	3,187
	8.10	Mount St. Helens		Southern Washington	8,365	2,550
2002	1.20	Caliente Peak, Caliente Ridge		Carrizo Plain, California	5,106	1,556
	2.24	Lookout Mountain		Argus Mountains, Death Valley NP	3,764	1,147
	4.21	Pinto Mountain		Joshua Tree NP	3,983	1,214
	5.1-3	Havasu Canyon, Beaver Falls		Havasupai Indian Reservation, Arizona		
	5.9	Angel's Landing		Zion NP	5,990	1,825
	7.2	Lembert Dome	1	Yosemite NP	9,450	2,880
	7.6	Arc Dome		Toiyabe Range, Central Nevada	11,773	3,588
2003	2.15	Newberry Peak		Rodman Wilderness Area, Southern California	5,117	1,560
	7.7	Mount Hoffman	2	Yosemite NP	10,850	3,307
2004	5.29	Gaylor Peak	1-2	Yosemite NP	11,004	3,354
	9.29	Frary Peak, Antelope Island		Great Salt Lake, Utah	6,596	2,010
	10.8	Deer Mountain		Rocky Mountain NP	10,013	3,052
2005	3.23	Camelback Mountain		Phoenix, Arizona	2,704	824
	3.29	Mastodon Peak		Joshua Tree NP	3,371	1,027
	5.19	Wildrose Peak		Death Valley NP	9,064	2,763
	5.23	Bright Angel Trail, three miles down		Grand Canyon NP		
2006	8.7	Liberty Pass		Ruby Mountains, Nevada	10,450	3,185

DATE		MOUNTAIN	CLASS	LOCATION	HEIGHT	
					Feet	Meters
2007	8.9	Gaylor Peak	1-2	Yosemite NP	11,004	3,354
2009	8.12	Pothole Dome		Tuolumne Meadows, Yosemite NP	8,766	2,672
	10.11	Weissenstein		Jura Mountains, Switzerland	4,580	1,396
2011	5.8	Top of the Potala Palace		Lhasa, Tibet	~13,100	~4,000

Countries Visited

Europe

1. Austria
2. Belgium
3. Croatia
4. Czech Republic
5. Denmark
6. East Germany
7. England
8. Estonia
9. Finland
10. France
11. Germany
12. Greece
13. Hungary
14. Iceland
15. Ireland
16. Italy
17. Liechtenstein
18. Monaco
19. Netherlands
20. Norway
21. Poland
22. Portugal
23. Romania
24. San Marino
25. Slovakia
26. Slovenia
27. Soviet Union
28. Spain
29. Sweden
30. Switzerland
31. Turkey
32. Ukraine
33. Vatican
34. Yugoslavia

Australia and Polynesia

1. Australia
2. Fiji
3. French Polynesia
4. New Zealand

North America

1. Canada
2. Mexico
3. United States*

Central America and the Caribbean

4. Belize
5. Bahamas
6. Costa Rica

7. Guatemala
8. Honduras
   Guadeloupe**
   Martinique**
   Virgin Islands**

South America

   Argentina***
9. Bolivia
10. Brazil
11. Chile
   Colombia***
12. Ecuador
   Galápagos Islands
13. Peru
14. Venezuela

Asia

1. Cambodia
2. China

3. Hong Kong
4. India
5. Israel
6. Japan
7. Malaysia
8. Nepal
9. Pakistan
   (Gilgit, Hunza)
10. Saudi Arabia
11. Singapore
12. Taiwan
13. Thailand
14. Tibet**
15. Vietnam

Africa

1. Kenya
2. South Africa
3. Tanzania

Notes on Countries and States

*All states except Alabama, Arkansas, Iowa, Nebraska, North Dakota, Oklahoma, Rhode Island, South Carolina, and South Dakota.

**May not be considered a separate country.

***Short visit of no more than a few hours.

I have visited a total of seventy countries, not including Argentina and Colombia, where I spent only a few hours to see Iguazu Falls and a *tepui* (table-top mountain). Spending about a week in each of them, I also visited a number of territories technically administered by foreign colonial powers: Guadeloupe (France),

Martinique (France), the US Virgin Islands, and Tibet (China). These may not be considered separate countries.

During the last century, new countries were created, other countries disappeared or were divided among successor states, some countries were united, and others became part of a larger country. The list shows the name of each country when I first visited there. For example, I was in Berlin before it was divided, when it was split between East and West, and again after the reunification of East and West Germany. I went to Hong Kong before it was returned to China. I was in the Czech Republic when parts of it belonged to Germany, but also in Czechoslovakia, before it split into the Czech Republic and Slovakia. Gabi and I were in Yugoslavia before it fell apart, and then in two of its successor states, Croatia and Slovenia.

Selected Publications of S. M. Csicsery

"Methylcyclopentadiene Isomers." *Journal of Organic Chemistry* (1960) 25, 518.

with Herman Pines, six publications on aromatization and dehydrocyclization over chromia alumina, *Chemistry and Industry* (1961), *Journal of American Chemical Society* (January and October 1962), *Journal of Catalysis* (January and August 1962), and *Journal of Chromatography A* (1962).

Reactions of n-Butylbenzene over Supported Platinum Catalysts." *Journal of Catalysis* (1967) 9, 336.

Five publications on catalyzed reactions of alkylaromatics. *Journal of Catalysis* (1967, 1968, and 1969).

Five publications on dehydrocyclodimerization, *Journal of Catalysis* (1970).

Three publications on shape selective transalkylation over mordenite catalysts. *Journal of Catalysis* (1970, 1971).

with Hugh F. Harnsberger, Walter D. Hughes, and Roger D. Searle. "Catalyst and Gas Samplers for Fluid Catalytic Cracker Regenerator." *Industrial and Engineering Chemistry Process Design and Development* (1975) 14, 93.

"Shape Selective Catalysis, Zeolite Chemistry and Catalysis." Chap. 12 (680–713) in *Zeolite Chemistry and Catalysis: ACS Monograph No. 171.* Edited by Jule A. Rabo. Washington, DC: American Chemical Society, 1976.

"Dehydrocyclodimerization." *Industrial and Engineering Chemistry Process Design and Development* (1979) 18, 191.

"Review: Shape Selective Catalysis in Zeolites." *Zeolites* (1984) 4, 202.

"Shape Selective Catalysis in Zeolites." *Chemistry in Britain* (1985) 21, 473.

"Fuel Processing Technology," in *New Developments in Zeolite Science and Technology: Proceedings of the 7th International Zeolite Conference, Tokyo, August 17–22, 1986*. Studies in Surface Science and Catalysis 28. Amsterdam: Elsevier; Tokyo: Kodansha, 1986.

Paál, Zoltán, and S. M. Csicsery, "Szénhidrogének Gyűrűzáródási Reakciói fém katalizátorokon." Chap 1 (7–199) in *A Kémia Újabb Eredményei*. Budapest: Akadémiai Kiadó, 1986.

Two publications on catalyst testing. *Journal of Catalysis* (1987, 1988).

Catalyst Testing: How and How Not to Test Catalysts. Spring House, PA: Catalyst Consultants, 1992.

Notes

1. This connection to the seven chiefs makes the Szemere family one of Hungary's oldest. The family's coat of arms shows a leg bent at the knee, in red pants and a black boot, on a blue shield, with a silver arrow piercing the knee, a gold star at the top right, and a silver crescent moon at the top left. A helmet with a closed crown sits over the shield. Above the crown is a drawn silver bow with a silver arrow. Below the shield, the words *De Genere Huba* appear in black letters on a silver ribbon. The silver arrow piercing the knee refers to Mihály Zemere, who was killed on April 12, 1241, in the battle of Mohi, in which the Mongols defeated the Hungarians.

   Over the centuries, the family split into numerous branches with estates in more than a dozen counties. Many family members reached prominent government positions, among them László Szemere, who was a general in Ferenc Rákóczi's rebel army in the early eighteenth century, and Bertalan Szemere, who became minister of interior in Kossuth's government in 1848. Two noteworthy ancestors, a Miklós and a Pál, were poets and writers, and both became members of the Hungarian Scientific Academy. Another Miklós, born in 1856, was a prominent gambler and racehorse breeder.

   Gabrielle has a copy of *Huba Vére—Szemere* [Huba's Blood—Szemere] by Gáspár Zarándy, a detailed history of her family published in 1910 by Viktor Hornyánszky in Budapest. It weighs some twelve pounds (5.5 kg).

2. Imre Samu, *A Szabács viadala* [The Battle of Szabács] (Budapest: Akadémiai Kiadó, 1958), 332.

3. László Oláh, *Két Levelesláda Vallomása Nyolc Évszázadról* [The Testimony of Two Cases of Archives Covering Eight Centuries] (Toronto: Vörösváry, 1992).

4. Of the 10,050,575 persons for whom Hungarian was the mother
   tongue in 1919, no fewer than 3,219,579 ended up in the successor states: 1,704,851 in Romania, 1,063,020 in Czechoslovakia,
   547,735 in Yugoslavia, and 26,183 in Austria. Sources: Károly
   Kocsis, Eszter Kocsisné Hodosi, *Ethnic Geography of the Hungarian Minorities in the Carpathian Basin* (TOWN: EXEN,
   1998) [2], 19; Uri Ra'anan, *State and Nation in Multi-Ethnic
   Societies: The Breakup of Multinational States* (Manchester, UK:
   Manchester University Press, 1991), 106.
5. Julián Borsányi, *Die Rätsel des Bombenangriffes auf Kassa: Ein
   dokumentarischer Bericht* [The Riddle of the Bombing of Kassa:
   a documentary report] (Munich: Verlag Dr. R.Tropenik, 1978).
6. James Bacque, *Other Losses* (Toronto: Stoddart, 1989).
7. Antal Csernavölgyi included my diary in his soldier-diary
   anthology. *Fegyvert, S Vitézt Éneklek: Katonanaplók a Háborúk-
   ból* [Of Weapons and Heroes I Sing: Soldier Diaries from the
   Wars] (Budapest: Logod Bt., 1997), 216–300.

   In 2011, Zala Films published the English translation of my
   diary. Sigmund Csicsery, *Almost a Soldier: The 1945 Diary of
   a Hungarian Cadet* (Oakland, CA: Zala Films, 2011). In 2011,
   I was awarded the Árpád Academy Gold Medal by the Szent
   László Rend, an international organization founded in Cleveland, Ohio in 1951, for the translation and publication of my
   diary.
8. In her book *Kitiltott Családok,* Zsuzsa Hantó provides detailed
   descriptions of the deportations. Zsuzsa Hantó, Kitiltott
   Családok (Budapest: Magyar Ház Kft., 2009). An English
   translation, *Banished Families. Communist Repression of "Class
   Enemies" in Hungary,* was published by the same company in
   the same year.
9. Géza Böszörményi and Lívia Gyarmathy, *Recsk 1950–1953,
   Egy titkos kényszermunkatábor története* (Recsk 1950–1953:
   The Story of a Secret Forced Labor Camp), 1989. A European
   Film Awards winner, this documentary tells the story of Recsk,
   Hungary's most notorious political prison camp, which oper-
   ated between 1950 and 1953. During the early 1950s, the very

existence of this camp at Recsk for political prisoners was one of the Hungarian Communist regime's deepest secrets. Hundreds of people were taken there without ever being sentenced by any court and had to suffer through brutal treatment by sadistic guards. The documentary tells the story of Recsk from both the captors' and the prisoners' point of view, portraying the atmosphere of paranoia, humiliation, and degradation that prevailed throughout the Stalinist gulag system.

10. *Szökés* (Escape) is a 1997 dramatic feature film directed by Lívia Gyarmathy, written by her husband, Géza Böszörményi, and starring Daniel Olbrychski, Krzysztof Kolberger, Artur Zmijewski, Adam Schnell, and László Zsolt. It is based on Böszörményi's own experiences as a young man sent to a prison camp for the crime of accidentally engaging in conversation with a fugitive. At the Recsk camp, he is put to work doing heavy manual labor and is given a starvation diet, just like the other prisoners. He joins seven men determined to escape, but is the only one to succeed. He has memorized the names of hundreds of his fellow prisoners, and once he escapes to the West, reads them over the air on Radio Free Europe.

11. On August 31, 1935, Aleksei Stakhanov, a miner working in the Donets Basin, hewed 102 tons of coal during his six-hour shift, a world record. This was fourteen times his quota. The Communist Party then launched the Stakhanovite movement. Workers and peasants who produced significantly more than their quota (norm) or otherwise excelled in their line became Stakhanovites. I received the Sztahanovista title twice, on August 1, 1952, and in April 1956. In August 1956, I was also named Kíváló Dolgozó (Outstanding Worker).

12. Károly Csonkaréti, *Szigorúan Titkos Dandár* [Strictly Secret Brigade], ed. Dr. Aniszi Kálmán (Budapest: Zrinyi Kiadó, Budapest, 1994).

13. Interrogators have been using this ruse for some time, as the Dominican inquisitor Nicholas Eymerich wrote in his *Directorium inquisitorum:* "To confront an unforthcoming prisoner, he might sit with a large stack of documents in front of him,

which he would appear to consult as he asked questions or listened to answers, periodically looking up from the pages as if they contradicted the testimony and saying, 'It is clear to me that you are hiding the truth.'" (Cullen Murphy, "Torturer's Apprentice," *The Atlantic*, January–February 2012: 71–77.)

14. From *A Magyar Nyelv Történeti-etimológiai Szótára* [Etymological Dictionary of the Hungarian Language], 1984.

15. From Magyar Értelmező kéziszótár [Hungarian Explanatory Dictionary], 1972.

16. Csicsery Zsigmond és társai; No. HB. VI. 854/1953.

17. Csicsery Zsigmond és társai; No. II. 639/1953.

18. Case No. VI. 499/1991.

19. Sigmund M. Csicsery, "Contribution to the Mechanism of Dehydrogenation, Dehydrocyclization and Dehydroisomerization of Hydrocarbons over Chromia-Alumina Catalysts." PhD diss. Northwestern University, 1962.

20. My most important accomplishments included the discovery of restricted transition state type shape selectivity (the nonobvious type of three types of shape selective catalytic reactions) and the invention of dehydrocyclodimerization, the reaction converting C_3-C_5 paraffins to BTX (i.e., C_6-C_8) aromatics.

21. Szilárd Szönyi, ed., *My Revolution: Recollections, 1956* (Budapest: Friends of Hungary Kft., 2016).

Made in the USA
San Bernardino, CA
17 September 2017